MARRIAGE
A REFLECTION OF GOD'S IMAGE

by SHAWN BAIN

ONE STONE
BIBLICAL RESOURCES

Published by:
One Stone Press
979 Lovers Lane
Bowling Green, KY 42103

Printed in the United States of America

ISBN 10: 0-9854938-2-8
ISBN 13: 978-0-9854938-2-0

Supplemental Materials Available:

➢ Power Point Slides for each lesson

➢ Downloadable PDF

➢ Downloadable Marriage Worksheet

www.onestone.com

ONE STONE
BIBLICAL RESOURCES

❧CONTENTS☙

Dedication

This humble effort I dedicate to my precious wife, Diane, an endless source of inspiration and

to the Southside Church of Christ in Somerset, KY, who first gave me the opportunity to teach

this material in a married couple's class during the Spring of 2013.

GUIDELINES FOR STUDY

- Genesis 2:18-25 is God's blueprint for every marriage and provides a starting point for discussion in this study.

- The reasons for this study are:

  1. To save marriages as designed by God. Various agendas of politics, social media, the homosexual movement, the Supreme Court, religious error, and society in general

  2. To know Christians are not exempt from marriage problems.

  3. To leave a legacy of a great marriage. This study benefits every couple, young or old. The current generation and the next generation need great, holy, and intimate marriages.

- Do the homework so the class will be productive and all will grow with their spouse in intimacy and spiritually.

- Make the commitment to your spouse to do the homework and to attend each class.

- Make class comfortable for a person to say what needs to be said, keeping what is heard in class discussion confidential.

- When a person gets emotional during a class while sharing something meaningful from the heart, do not interrupt by giving a hug or making a comment. (i.e. rescuing)

- Keep these 3 things in mind: HONESTY, TRUST, CONFIDENTIALITY

- Promise to keep everything confidential a person might decide to share. People need to feel safe. Questions asked or comments made do not indicate a marriage problem.

- There is to be no spouse trashing! No sarcastic comments permitted.

- Commit to improving your relationship with your spouse, not change them. If change takes place, let it be in you. When you read or hear a point in class, do not think of your spouse, think of yourself. Let Jesus change you!

- Realize your marriage is a point of evangelism and can lead others to the Lord. What people hear and see in your marriage often prompts others to know how your marriage is so peaceful, loving, caring, honorable, etc

- Before reading this material, complete this sentence. Marriage is _____. Allow those in the class to share their answer as a way to begin your discussion of the material in this book. By the end of the class, see if your thoughts of marriage have changed or remained the same.

MARRIAGE IN THE IMAGE OF GOD

A. Where Do You Get Marriage Advice?

1. Seeking marriage advice from certain people is not always the best thing, especially from THOSE WITH TROUBLED OR BROKEN MARRIAGES. Some divorced people, if they are self-reflecting and not selfish, spend time thinking about what went wrong. It is "marriage advice learned the hard way." Those who evaluate their mistakes identify five behaviors they believe contributed to the demise of their marriage. They are:

    a. Not boosting your spouse's mood. They would give their spouse more "affective affirmation," which includes compliments, cuddling, kissing, hand-holding, saying "I love you," and emotional support. It would build trust. Trust they did not achieve in their marriage.

    b. Not talking more about money. Money was the number one point of conflict in the majority of marriages. Many couples had different spending styles, lied about spending, or tried to control the other. This behavior caused a lack of trust. Six out of ten divorced people, who began a new relationship, chose not to combine finances.

    c. Not getting over the past. Any relationship that hinders a positive outcome would be included. This includes jealousy of a spouse's past relationships, irritation at how your in-laws treat you, anger from a previous spat with your spouse, and unresolved childhood issues.

    d. Not taking ownership. Many of the divorced blamed the cause on anxiety, depression, sleep disorders, and other personal maladies. Others

Your **relationship to God** is a **good sign** of what your **relationship** is with **your spouse**.

God does not look to **make** your marriage an **"average marriage"**. His desire is for **your marriage** to **reflect His image** and parallel with the relationship of Christ and the church...

blamed their spouse's angry moods, personal habits, attitudes, and "he never...he always," or "she never...she always."

e. Not revealing more about self. Most divorced individuals said they would add more communication to their "next relationship" (41% said they would communicate differently). They would "actively listen" and truly hear what the other person is saying, be more open and honest, and take time to learn more about their mate rather than assume they knew enough.

2. THOSE IN A MARITAL RELATIONSHIP have some advice, too.

a. "We've always done things together. We did not have a lot of money, but we had lots of good times. We always eat together, pray together, and serve together," (Fred and Patricia - 56 yrs).

b. "People have to enjoy their partner for their gifts and abilities rather than look for their faults. It is important to respond to the needs of your spouse. We may be tired and not feel like taking care of each other, but we give it all we have," (Harold and Lanniece - 27 years).

c. "The single most influential thing in our relationship that keeps us together and focused is our commitment to our family. When things get rough between us, we remember our family and we get on track. To keep our relationship strong, we laugh at ourselves, each other, and our situations," (Marlin and Lorna - 8 years).

d. "We make time at least once a week to go for a walk or a bike ride to a nearby park. We also set one evening each week aside to talk and relax together, and the two of us make time for each other after we have put the children to bed," (Carlos and Norma - 10 years).

e. "Live each day with and for your mate as if it were the only day you had together," (Leon and Dorothy - 48 years.)

f. What marriage advice would you give to other married couples, and what do you believe are

the ingredients of a successful marriage? _____
_____
_____

B. The Best Marriage Advice Comes from God.

1. Read Genesis 2:18-25 and Ephesians 5:22-33. What is God advising us to consider about marriage in these texts? _____
_____
_____
_____

2. If you were given a plan, a "stimulus package" for your marriage and put it into action, knowing things would be better, love greater, union stronger, then you would praise and laud its effect on your marriage. Here it is! It is a God created, designed, and advised marriage package.

3. KNOW THIS: Although God has the best advice for your marriage, it is your choice as to where your marriage is today! It's your way or His way. Have you really read, reviewed, meditated, and put into practice God's plan and the things which (1) make marriage, (2) benefit marriage, and (3) improve marriage. Most people have not.

4. Marriage is like a puzzle with pieces to put together. We need God's help in putting these pieces together to make our marriage EXCELLENT. Yes, excellent. God does not look to make your marriage an "average marriage." His desire is for your marriage to reflect His image and parallel with the relationship of Christ and the church.

5. What does Philippians 1:9,10 say our commitment should be? _____
_____

C. God's Blueprint for Marriage - Genesis 2:18-25.

1. You know why you married, and why you married the person you did. It may have been for companionship, sex, security, similar interests, or to have children, etc. Whatever the reason, we need to know why God designed marriage and what it should be.

2. What plan does God have for making your marriage work? Note the following:

   a. Fulfill loneliness (v.18). This not only covers the fact man has no companion to which he can relate and share, but it shows the dependence of man upon God to help him be what he can be. Man needs God to help resolve his loneliness.

      1. Your relationship to God is a good sign of what your relationship is with your spouse. If you have isolated yourself from God, you have probably isolated yourself from your mate.

2.   To be a great mate, first make your relationship with God what it ought to be. Read and study how those in the New Testament heard, believed, repented, and were baptized to be one with God (Acts 2:27-41; Ephesians 2:15-16). Living without God in your life and in your marriage is "aloneness" that is not good.

b.   **Acceptance of Spouse (v.21-23).** How was Adam going to receive Eve? "She's okay...just my size...pretty hair..." The man expresses a deep, rich appreciation for this gift. "This is bone of my bones, flesh of my flesh, she shall be called Woman..." God wants you to receive, respect, and rejoice in the spouse He custom made for you! God is to be trusted. What words of "acceptance" could you say to your spouse indicating you accept him/her as a gift from God? _____

_____

_____

c.   **Leave Others for Your Spouse (v.24; Matthew 19:5).** This scripture commands us to leave our parents and their household. We also need to leave other relationships with men/women, past abuses, mistakes, habits, toys, etc. Some may need to leave or abandon influences from their parents' marriage because those influences may affect your marriage negatively.

1.   Never "leave" or isolate yourself from your spouse emotionally, physically, spiritually, or intimately (Note 1 Corinthians 7:1-5). Some have taken on jobs, hobbies, and other relationships with people causing them to slowly leave their mate.

2.   In what ways do you believe a spouse "leaves" his/her mate in marriage (i.e. isolates or withdraws from their spouse)? _____

_____

_____

d.   **Cleave (v.24).** Permanence is God's plan for your union. Two people marry and form a commitment, a bond, a covenant, pledging to the other for a lifetime. You grab hold with firmness as Matthew 19:6 says. It is at this point where accountability begins. You made vows before God and it is good to review them, write them down, or recite them again to your spouse. It will be evident to you and your spouse what you promised.

1.   You need to pray about this commitment every day. The love shared at a wedding is not a guarantee love will always be there. You need strength from God to cleave to each other every day in the marriage. If you cleave today, it makes cleaving tomorrow a bit easier.

2.   The more one cleaves, the more "one-fleshed" a couple becomes: physically, emotionally, spiritually, and intimately.

e.   **Intimacy—Openness and Honesty (v.25).** Intimacy is what God has in mind for marriage. The sexual union has its part here, but before sexual oneness takes place, intimacy of the heart (emotional intimacy) must be present.

1. God's design for "one flesh" is for a couple to not be ashamed emotionally. There are no barriers, no skeletons, or covering up, but sharing your life with each other.

2. Being "real" with each other establishes trust which takes marriage from an emotional level to a sexual level. There will not be a problem with physical intimacy in marriage if the emotional intimacy is there.

3. The true aspect of "lovemaking" is the revealing of heart, spirit, emotions, will, and body. This is part of the purity and sanctification of your marriage.

   f. This blueprint is not optional. This is God's design. His image is to be reflected in your marriage. Following this pattern is a "signpost" pointing to the way God wants you to be rather than spending all your married life thinking it is about you. Marriage is the "signpost" telling us the direction our life needs to go—toward God.

3. At this moment, what does your marriage reveal about God to you? _____

   _____

   _____

4. From studying Genesis 2:18-25, how does marriage reflect the image of God?

   _____

   _____

   _____

5. What aspect of God's character would you most like your marriage to reveal to the world? _____

   _____

6. What can you do to accomplish this in your marriage? _____

   _____

D. The Impact of Your Marriage.

1. Personal affect of marriage. There was no shame when Adam and Eve were joined together (Genesis 2:25). When sin came into their marriage (Genesis 3:7,8), they covered up, hid, and were ashamed; blame and criticism erupted. Sin affected their relationship with God and each other.

   a. If sin exists in your marriage, you will be ashamed, critical, angry, deceptive, isolated and lonely. You will have ruined God's plan for oneness in marriage.

   b. Sin in marriage affects us personally. It takes man to a feeling of pride and independence, rather than dependence on God. When you take God out of the picture, marriage fails.

2. Societal affect of marriage. Adam and Eve's marriage laid the foundation of what people need to know about marriage and the value of a good relationship. Your marriage has an impact on others.

a. When sin entered their marriage, death entered the world (Genesis 3:3,4; Romans 5:12). The responsibilities of labor, child bearing, headship, and submission began. Their marriage affected all of creation.

b. Someone's marriage has already affected you. Your marriage will impact someone else besides you.

c. Marriages influence a church and become one factor in choosing an elder or deacon.

d. Your marriage is the foundation of the family, community, and nation. The attitudes that develop in your marriage are also witnessed in a church, school, community, and the next generation.

3. There is hope for marriage. Genesis 3:15 provides hope for man to be redeemed from sin. It is a plan God created. Therefore, man does not have to end his life hopeless in spiritual death. There is also hope for marriage. As a soul can be "born again" (John 3:5), so can a marriage. Marriage, as God designed, is worth having and keeping. Do not allow Satan to divide and frustrate you, but prevent him from doing so by becoming one with God, and therefore one with your mate. Let God create you and your marriage into a reflection of His image.

4. From studying the effect Adam and Eve's marriage had on them personally and others, what would you do to protect your marriage from Satan so it would not have a negative effect on you, your family, the church, and society? _____
_____
_____

E. Image Builders for Your Marriage.

1. Develop a five-year plan for your marriage. Make it simple, not lengthy, and have it mirror what pleases God. Set aside a time and place for you and your spouse to discuss how your plan can reflect the image of God. Use some godly marriages in the Bible as your guide.

2. List three things you would put in your plan for the next 5 years. _____
_____
_____

3. Which married couple in the Bible would be your "marriage example" and why? _____
_____
_____

4. Write a short letter to your spouse stating why you have accepted them unconditionally.

5. "The bonds of matrimony are a good investment only when the interest is kept."

6. "Trouble in marriage often starts when a man gets so busy earnin' his salt, he forgets his sugar."

NOTES:

SPIRITUAL INTIMACY IN MARRIAGE - THE FORGOTTEN INTIMACY

A. Most couples long for a "marriage made in heaven." It comes with love, closeness, affection, discovery, and joy. This would be a successful marriage. When people talk about having a godly marriage, what does this mean? __

_____

B. How would you rate your spiritual relationship with your mate? 1 – 10 (1=poor; 10=excellent) _____

C. It is relatively easy to understand the emotional intimacy that creates a heart-to-heart bond as well as the physical intimacy that brings a couple together body-to-body. Also, every couple needs a soul-to-soul closeness. If you want to enjoy the deepest level of connection, then you need to develop spiritual intimacy in your relationship.

D. The true success of your marriage depends on whether it is experiencing *spiritual intimacy*. It is the most important part in a marriage, but it is the most forgotten. It is the intimacy which brings richness and honor to all the other intimacies in marriage. A couple marries "before God," yet fails to take God into their life and marriage. As a result, a couple deceives themself and appears in a worship service with a stain-glass, go-to-church, "spit-shine" look. The God who joined them together is the same God who will keep them from parting asunder (Matthew 19:4-6).

> A couple **marries "before God,"** yet **fails to take God** into their life and marriage.

E. Every couple should understand that the *reflection of God* in their marriage is a daily assignment to become close to God, and therefore close to one another (Psalm 27:1-6). If your personal spiritual life lacks love, devotion, zeal, and courage, then your marriage will be deficient in all the same categories.

F. When a spouse grows in their relationship with God, he/she begins to think like God thinks. When a couple thinks like God in their marriage, he/she pleases God in their responsibility to marriage and pleases their spouse. When both think like God, they become so united and close, "they think alike."

G. Why Is Spiritual Intimacy Important?

1. What kind of trouble did the relationship of Adam and Eve encounter in the garden (Genesis 3)? Was it a spiritual problem or just a communication problem? _____
   _____
   _____

2. Jeremiah 2 tells us of a woman's desire for love. She delighted in a man as the man delighted in her. Her commitment to him was tested when she was enticed by the passion, thrill, and adventure of another lover (Jeremiah 2:33). This woman represents the nation of Israel. She turned from her commitment to God, forsook His love and pursued other relationships. Every couple should pursue and be attracted to the ONE they are pledged to for life—both God and their spouse.

3. To teach Israel a lesson about intimacy with Him, God had Hosea marry Gomer (Hosea 1). Gomer's children were given names indicating a spiritual connection to "the house of Israel" (1:6,9). Some of those children were born from an adulterous relationship and this was not what God wanted from Israel. In Hosea 3, God had Hosea take Gomer back and "Love a woman." This was to show him God's love for Israel. God used his marriage to provide a spiritual lesson.

4. Jesus talked about "an adulterous generation," an unacceptable relationship (Mark 8:38). The only relationship God desired was with Him, not another. A man and woman's relationship is defined by the two becoming ONE relationship, not multiple relationships.

5. Why does God make a parallel of marriage to Christ and the church in Ephesians 5:22-33? _____
   _____
   _____
   _____
   _____

6. In many ways, all these references to marriage are defining the spirituality of marriage. This makes

If you push spiritual intimacy to the back burner, off to the side, you are ignoring the very **God** Who **created marriage** and the **One Who can help** you make it work.

marriage a way to avoid sexual immorality, populate the world, and end man's loneliness. Marriage is a holy, sacred, honorable, and consecrated place.

7. Every couple should understand their marriage is first and foremost a spiritual relationship. "Shall two walk together, except they have agreed" (Amos 3:3) is not only a principle for a couple where one is a Christian and the other is not. It applies to Christians married to one another, who should see their marriage will not excel and grow unless they agree to be spiritually intimate with God.

8. Matthew 7:24-27 finds Jesus talking about the need to build one's spiritual house on solid ground by obeying God. A house on the rock can withstand the floods of doubt, winds of change, and rising immoral trends. A couple who is not spiritually founded upon God will not be prepared for the storms which will assault their marriage (care for elderly parent, lost job, disease, blindness, etc.).

9. Psalms 127:1 says, "Except the _____ _____ the _____, they labor in vain that build it."

10. If you push spiritual intimacy to the back burner, off to the side, you are ignoring the very God who created marriage and the One who can help you make it work. Instead of saying, "I want to have a happy marriage," you should say, "I want to have a holy marriage ." This is a marriage made in heaven.

H. The Spiritual TRIANGLE of Marriage.

1. Most marriages are based upon a horizontal relationship of a husband and wife. Their relationship is often viewed as 50/50 with a give-and-take, meet me half-way feeling. Most "half-way" marriages end up being selfishly driven, wanting more from the other than they are willing to give.

Husband ◄————————► Wife

2. Considering the diagram to the right, if one spouse draws close to God and the other spouse does not, the distance between the couple is still the same. The couple never becomes closer in ONEness to God or with their spouse. As each spouse strives to be closer to God, they become closer to one another, increasing the love, and increasing ONEness. You grow together spiritually when you live your marriage relationship according to God's ways and aim to please Him in all things.

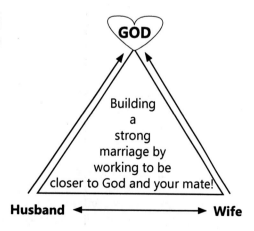

3. In consideration of this illustration, what would you advise a person to do as a faithful Christian in a "spiritually uneven" marriage? _____

_____

_____

_____

4. Based on the illustration, there is no reason to accept anything less in your marriage. To do so is to accept something less than what God provides for you in marriage. Every couple should be like Acts 11:23 "with _____ of _____ they would _____ unto the Lord..."

5. Spiritual intimacy is a heart's desire to be close to God and His direction. As a result, you become closer to your spouse.

I. Why Does Spiritual Intimacy Not Exist in Marriage?

1. Ironically, spiritual intimacy in marriage does not come easy to many Christians. Some Christians speak of it being "uncomfortable." The spirit is willing, but the flesh is weak (Matthew 26:41). We love the Lord, but we cannot learn about and pray to the Lord together. Therefore, we become easy pickins' for Satan or settle for "second best" in our marriage.

2. What are some things inhibiting/prohibiting you from developing spiritual intimacy? _____

_____

_____

3. Here are some ways to detect if your marriage lacks spiritual maturity.

   a. Your marriage experiences conflicts in many areas. You frequently disagree about a variety of subjects. Some subjects you label "off limits" or "you don't go there" subjects. You intentionally avoid them.

   b. You feel incomplete. There is "just something missing." You are having a hard time "putting a finger on it."

   c. You lack a firm foundation for your marriage commitment. You may have promised "until death we do part", but your commitment lacks what will keep it permanent – your personal devotion to God. Your marriage will become an arrangement of convenience rather than commitment. When it is no longer convenient, you will give up, become distracted by other things, and want out.

   d. You lack boundaries for guarding your marriage. The Bible provides absolute standards for right and wrong and God's people delight in those commands. When you do not discipline yourself, your marriage is no longer protected from other people and things.

   e. You "do not have time" for spiritual things. "We have more pressing needs right now." When the smallest of concerns are pressing and urgent, spiritual intimacy is often the first thing pushed off the list. Without time for God, you fail to make time for your spouse.

f.   You are afraid of honesty and openness. James 5:16 is very personal, honest, and open about relationships. Some couples do not talk about nor trust their mate with money, places they go, who they see, what they watch, who they call, etc. Some spouses do not allow their life to be exposed to their mate. As a result, they do not submit to one another spiritually (Ephesians 5:21), because spiritual intimacy exposes them for who they really are and the mistakes they have made.

g.   You are ashamed or embarrassed. When there is shame, there is fear your mate will laugh, criticize, or reject you. Who says your spouse will not love you because you are open, honest, and pleasing God? Because of shame we say,"I'm tired," "It's late," or "Not right now." In other words, we are hiding what is in our heart. You already feel like a hypocrite, so why expose yourself to more hurt and pain.

h.   You believe your spouse is "not interested in spiritual matters." If your spouse is struggling with spiritual intimacy, pray for him or her. Share your convictions, if your spouse will listen, then let God's word work. As you obey the scriptural command to win them by a "gentle and quiet spirit" (1 Peter 3:4), you allow God to open their spiritual eyes. God will work in your mate's heart as you treat him or her "with understanding" (1 Peter 3:7). You can be God's instrument in reaching your spouse.

i.   You are in sin. "I know I should talk with my wife about spiritual things," a husband said to me, "but when our relationship isn't right in other areas, it feels hypocritical to start talking about God and the Bible." If you are involved in lying, cheating, or seeing something you should not, you are not going to take the hand of your spouse and pray or open a Bible and read together. Think about what sin did to the marriage of Adam and Eve, Abraham and Sarah, David and Bathsheba, Hosea and Gomer, Ahab and Jezebel.

4.   Which of the following "inhibitors to spiritual intimacy" affect your life the most?

a. busyness   e. low-level anger, small conflicts
b. lack of forgiveness   f. spiritual warfare
c. lack of spiritual zeal   g. other_____
d. lack of respect

J. Spiritual Intimacy in Your Marriage Begins When...?

1.   You and your spouse turn to God together, asking Him to help you build total intimacy in your marriage, no matter how spiritually inadequate you believe you are. When both husband and wife come to the cross of Christ, both are on level ground. Spiritual growth in your marriage is not just knowing more about the Bible, it is becoming more like Christ. Be open to allow Christ to work in your life.

2. You are being a God-centered spouse rather than a spouse-centered spouse. A couple often views their situation and says: "We need to communicate better," "We need to compliment and appreciate one another more," "We need to better handle conflict," "We need to work more at being romantic". Those changes may need to be made, but most couples make an exchange to accomplish what they see is deficient.

   a. A spouse-centered spouse acts nice toward the husband when he acts nice to her and gives her attention. Then, she accommodates him and is affectionate. He will romance her as long as he is rewarded.

   b. NOTE: Marriage does not call us to love our spouse because he/she makes us feel gooey inside. You are called to love, regard and honor your spouse in reverence to God, not for self-gratification. We are called to holiness, love, forgiveness, kindness, etc. regardless of our spouse's repsonse (Colossians 3:8-15).

   c. Every decision I make, every word I utter, every thought I think, every movement I perform, is to flow out of one holy motivation—reverence for God.

   d. This calling from God in marriage is spiritually motivated, not physically motivated, and results in spiritual intimacy. As a result, you become what is needed because you are centered on what God wants you to be (2 Corinthians 7:1).

3. You talk about it. Spiritual intimacy grows when a couple talks and listens during discussions about spiritual matters. Talk about what God can do and is doing in your marriage. Discuss with each other what you found encouraging or insightful in a sermon or passage. Do not preach to your spouse because this does not enhance spiritual intimacy. On occasions, ask your spouse to pray for you about some of the ways God wants you to be more spiritually minded.

4. You pray together. One man said he knew of no couple who proceeded with a divorce after praying together every day for a week. In the book "When Couples Pray Together," according to Dave and Jan Stoops, 4% of couples pray together regularly. Of the couples who pray together, 1 out of 1200 divorce.

   a. Prayer provides a richness and depth to marriage and intimacy. The experience of praying together unites hearts, helping you feel closer to each other and God. Few spiritual exercises hold as great a potential for spiritual intimacy as praying together. It brings growth to your communication, with an understanding of each other, and reduces selfishness.

   b. Prayer is where you do not hide! It is pouring out your heart and life to God. It allows you to say things your spouse may not hear you say at any other time. There should not be anything you would not want your mate to see or hear. Seek God together. Ask God for His grace to allow you to grow old together.

c. Do not allow mealtime prayers to become your means of spiritual intimacy. Find the time and place to pray together other than at the kitchen table. If you are uncomfortable praying aloud in the presence of another person, hold hands, close your eyes, and pray silently. (NOTE: Part of leadership as a husband is to lead your wife in prayer.) Pray for each other daily. Pray for the concerns your spouse has shared with you. Pray for spiritual wisdom and power (Ephesians 1:15-23; Philippians 1:9-11). What do you believe would happen to your marriage if you prayed together? _____

_____

_____

_____

_____

5. You have a devotion together. You can study a Bible subject or particular Bible text. A devotional book (EX: "Moments With You" by Dennis and Barbara Rainey) has daily lessons that can be discussed. Share one thing about the Bible text or devotion that impresses you.

6. You serve God together. Worship together, be given to hospitality, help a widow, visit the sick or those in the hospital, teach a class at your house, send out announcements and invite others to worship services, or take some young people on an outing together.

7. You see your marriage as a spiritual adventure. Pay attention to what helps your spouse grow spiritually. Encourage your spouse to pursue those activities. Understand what CAN be and IS being done in your marriage to make it grow spiritually. Continue to do it.

8. You have Jesus on the throne ruling and leading. Follow Him. Fall in love with God so you can fall in love with each other. Falling in love is a life, a life found in Galatians 5:16,17. Let your marriage realize through spiritual intimacy "_____ is he that is in_____, than _____ that is in the _____," (1 John 4:4).

Spiritual intimacy removes pride, ego, isolation, and deception. It creates attachment, intimacy, ONENESS, emotional and physical connection, trust, honesty, closeness, peace, safety, mercy, love, joy, and hope.

Spiritual intimacy in marriage is discovering what God wants you to be for your mate. It is also your spouse discovering how to help you please God. Spiritual intimacy is an act of commitment. It is an act of the will in which a husband and wife decide to walk together and with the help of God grow toward intimacy—emotionally, physically, sexually and spiritually.

If you refuse to bring spiritual intimacy into your marriage, it means you refuse to take your marriage to a higher level of appreciation, respect, and devotion.

If spiritual intimacy is a problem in your marriage consider the following suggestions:

a. If it is a "TIMING ISSUE," find the time—determine it.

b. Find the place to have time for spiritual intimacy.

  c. Find the subject—what to study.

  d. Once you start and see how close you are becoming with your spouse, DO NOT STOP!

There are many examples of couples we have witnessed, including our own, which have benefitted from spiritual intimacy. Here is a biblical example: Aquila and Priscilla (Acts 18:1-3, 18, 26; Romans 16:3-4). What did Aquila and Priscilla do together which increased spiritual intimacy in their marriage? _____
_____

Remember the Spiritual Intimacy Triangle! Spiritual intimacy is the truth of allowing your marriage to reflect the image of God.

K. Image Builders for Your Marriage.

  1. What five things can you do as A COUPLE to bring spiritual intimacy into your marriage? _____
   _____

  2. What are the benefits of developing spiritual intimacy with your spouse? What are the dangers of not doing so? _____
   _____
   _____
   _____

  3. Find a married couple in the Bible who you consider to be spiritually intimate in their marriage. What do you believe they did to develop a spiritually intimate marriage? _____
   _____
   _____

  4. One idea to bring about spiritual intimacy in your marriage is to discuss with each other what has been your greatest joy of the week and what has been

   your greatest struggle of the week. _____
   _____
   _____
   _____

  5. Ten Principles to Keep Christ at the Center of Your Home.

   a. Remember the Builder (Hebrews 3:4).

   b. Seek knowledge (Colossians 1:9).

   c. Be on the alert for evil (1 Peter 5:8).

   d. Follow God's directions (Psalm 119:15, 54).

e.   Live in ONEness (Mark 3:25).

f.   Seek understanding (Proverbs 24:3-4).

g.   Develop character values. Who you are is what your family becomes (Galatians 5:22,23).

h.   Ask God to help and choose every day to serve the Lord (Joshua 24:15).

i.   Remember the Master of your home [the Lord] will return (Mark 13:34-35).

j.   Have a vision for your marriage (Proverbs 29:18).

NOTES:

REFLECTING ON EACH OTHER - THE NEEDS OF MARRIAGE

A. For the first time in U.S. history, single adults outnumber married adults for people between ages of 25 – 34, (Population Reference Bureau, 2010). For those married, over 40% will end in divorce. Between 25 - 50% of Americans commit adultery. Three out of four Americans have premarital sex before the age of 20. Over half of all first marriages are now preceded by cohabitation. Those who cohabit before marriage have a higher divorce risk than those who do not. Couples who cohabitate before marriage report less marital happiness and more conflict when married. Marriage in America and around the world needs something. What does it NEED? _____

_____

_____

_____

_____

B. Many couples do not need a new understanding of marriage, they NEED to understand marriage needs them. Some believe changing spouses is the answer. The divorce rate for second marriages is higher than first marriages—60%! Therefore, if the level of your marriage has reached an all time stale level, you NEED a new marriage with the same spouse.

C. For HUSBANDS only: Why do men need marriage? ____

_____

_____

_____

D. For WIVES only: Why do women need marriage? _____

_____

_____

_____

God created man with a **NEED** for **intimacy**.

Regardless of what **your mate needs** from you and what **you need** from your mate, you must **accept them** as they are, **without conditions** attached.

E.   The NEED in the Beginning.

1.   Read Genesis 2:18-23. What NEEDS do you believe God intended a marriage to fulfill? (Give at least four.) _____
_____
_____

2.   God wanted to fulfill man's aloneness. There was no creature for man (Genesis 2:18-21).

3.   The word ALONE in the Hebrew means bad. It is as if God wanted man to see it was bad to be alone. The word alone also means besides, a part. This shows man was a part of the whole, part of something not existing in totality.

4.   God created man with a NEED for intimacy. Intimacy is the process in which two caring people share as freely as possible in the exchange of feelings, thoughts and actions, marked by a mutual sense of acceptance, commitment, tenderness and trust. Man NEEDED to share himself with someone, but there was no creature in all the animals God made to satisfy this NEED. Every creature had a mate except man. When God made woman, the help meet (helpmate – in the Hebrew meaning someone to correspond, match), then the process was completed. She completed man and he completed her. This was demonstrated in the words of the man when he said, "this is now bone of my bones and flesh of my flesh" (v.23).

5.   Compare man's need for a mate with what God knows the church needs. Read 1 Corinthians 12:20-25. Does God need every Christian to understand the function of other members of the body? _____

6.   A couple admits their NEED for each other while they are dating and at their wedding. When a crisis enters the relationship, instead of expressing the need to our spouse, we isolate ourselves and withdraw from the one who can help us the most. Then, comes "I don't love her any more," or "I don't need him anymore."

7.   Ephesians 4:15 says, "...speaking truth in love may grow up in all things into him." You need to grow up, speak the truth with love and express your need for your spouse. Question is, does your spouse know why you NEED him/her and what NEEDS you have.

If you were asked the three greatest needs of your spouse, would you know what they are and how to fulfill each need? Most couples do not know the answer to this question.

8. FOR HUSBANDS ONLY: As a husband, do you believe it is important to know the NEEDS of your wife? If so, why? _____
_____
_____

9. FOR WIVES ONLY: As a wife, do you believe it is important to know the NEEDS of your husband? If so, why? _____
_____

10. Consider the following ways you NEED your spouse.

   a. For a balanced and truthful viewpoint of yourself (Galatians 6:1; James 5:19,20). Who can give you an honest perspective when you need it most and still offer you acceptance?

   b. To believe in you when others don't and you can't (Romans 12:3-6). God knows what you can do. Your spouse gives you expectancy, praise, and belief making you feel significant.

   c. To multiply your joys, divide your sorrows (1 Corinthians 12:25,26; Galatians 6:2). You need someone to share your successes and comfort you when things are rough. There is an understanding heart with your mate.

   d. To raise spiritually and physically healthy children (Ephesians 6:2-4; 2 Timothy 3:15). There is nothing greater than a husband and wife who are diligent, prayerful, and joyful in raising children together.

   e. To make you laugh, feel secure, bring warmth to your heart, give organization to your life, talk to you, listen to you, share with you, and make you feel important. He/she is the person with whom you want to spend the rest of your life. You long to be needed and not go through life alone.

F. Do I Deserve Marriage My Way?

   1. Burger King once advertised—Have It Your Way. Would the same idea reap a holy marriage? _____

   2. When a couple's marriage reaches the point it needs help, they will say, "I'll do anything to make our marriage work." Some will discuss their problem, but really want to know more about what the other spouse is supposed to do rather than learning his/her own duties and how to fulfill the other person's needs.

   3. At one time or another, all of us have experienced the feeling that our needs in marriage are not being met. Why doesn't she/he understand I need _____? All I want him/her to do is _____. If she/he would just _____. Why isn't he/she making me happy? If he/she would do their part, I would do mine! Most often the final conclusion is He/She just does not understand.

4. When those needs are not met, a spouse will become dissatisfied, bitter, fearful, hurt, lonely, resentful and frustrated. Why does this dilemma exist? The answer is simple—SELFISHNESS.

G. Our Need for God.

1. Read Matthew 19:16-24. People today, like the rich ruler, feel something is lacking. They are in need. The word *lack* means "come too late, to fall short, suffer need, in want of." He was asking Jesus, "In what way am I still less than I need to be?"

2. We have all felt we are missing something. You wish the Lord was sitting right there with you telling you what you lack (need). Some marriages today are just lacking. Couples will say, "We go to church together, work hard, and are good people, but our marriage needs something."

3. What does Hebrews 11:6 say *pleases* God? _____
_____

4. Why then is it so many people *displease* God? _____
_____

5. Complete this sentence. What God needs from us is _____
_____

6. Our first need should be for God. We understand the humility and selflessness needed to have fellowship with God. The desire to be intimate with God leads to intimacy with your mate.

7. God fills your needs. You are never unfulfilled with God (Ephesians 3:20; 2 Peter 1:3). God has met every physical *need* (Matthew 6:33,34; Philippians 4:6,7); the *need* for security (Romans 8:35-39); the *need* for purpose (Ecclesiastes 12:13; Ephesians 2:10); and the *need* for life (John 4:14; 10:10)

8. Christians never operate in emptiness, but in fullness because in Christ we are full (Colossians 2:9,10). Any disciple who *hungers and thirsts for righteousness shall be filled* (Matthew 5:6).

9. Consider what Psalm 107:8,9 says satisfies *the longing soul.*

10. Those who do not allow God to fulfill those needs become indifferent, empty, rebellious, dissatisfied, confused, and unbelieving. These are similar to the attitudes of a marriage where needs are not met.

11. It is imperative for God to fill our life, but why does a marriage NEED God? __
_____
_____
_____

H. What My Marriage NEEDS from Me?

1. God told Cain, *sin coucheth at the door* (Genesis 4:7). Since sin is so close and wants to destroy your marriage, it is time for every husband and wife to:

    a. Remind myself every morning, I am in a spiritual battle for my marriage and home. Begin each day asking myself, *Who will be at the center of my marriage today-Christ or me?* (James 3:15-17)

    b. Remember to intentionally follow the words of Philippians 2:3. Ask your spouse daily what you can do for them.

    c. Continually offer my spouse forgiveness (Matthew 5:7).

    d. Rely upon God's understanding of what my marriage needs (Proverbs 3:5, Ephesians 5:22-33).

    e. Review often the words of 1 Corinthians 13:4-8a. Your marriage deserves LOVE this way. By this, all men will know your marriage reflects the image of God (John 13:34,35).

2. Read Colossians 3:5-14. From this passage, what attitudes and behaviors does marriage need and not need? _____
    _____
    _____

3. Here is something every spouse needs to know. If the needs of your mate are not met, your spouse will seek the fulfillment of those needs with another person or thing.

4. Are your needs in marriage the same as your spouse's needs? Why or why not? _____
    _____

5. Do the needs of your spouse ever change or do they remain the same? Why or why not? _____
    _____
    _____

6. Meditate on these three important thoughts.

    a. Regardless of what your mate needs from you and what you need from your mate, you must accept them as they are, without conditions attached.

    b. Examine carefully the need you are asking your spouse to fulfill. Is it meant to force them to change? Are you asking something reasonable and within their capability to do?

    c. Pray for attention, understanding, patience, and wisdom as you help fulfill your mate's needs.

I.   Image Builders for Your Marriage.

1.   Each husband and wife should create a "Needs of Marriage" sheet using one sheet of paper like the example to the right. The front page should look like "Side A" and the back page should look like "Side B." This sheet is available for free download at www.onestone.com.

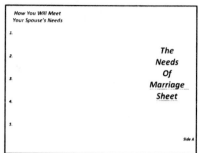

Each husband and wife takes time to complete this sheet and share their information with their spouse. Instead of a husband or wife thinking or saying, "I know what he/she needs," this exercise gives each spouse knowledge of what their spouse needs without guessing or misunderstanding.

a.   Take the sheet and fold it as a tri-fold. Make sure the words "The Needs of Marriage Sheet" is on the front. The inside page should read "Your Needs." The second sheet should read "How Your Spouse Will Meet Your Needs." The back side of the third page should read "How You Will Meet Your Spouse's Needs."

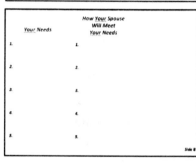

b.   Both will list five needs they have in marriage. Then, each states the ways they believe their spouse can meet the corresponding need on the sheet "How Your Spouse Will Meet Your Needs." After completing, fold the page "How You Will Meet Your Spouse's Needs" over the second page. Hand your list to your spouse.

c.   Your spouse will see the mate's Needs List and the sheet "How You Will Meet Your Spouse's Needs." Looking at the Needs List, you will write down how you will meet each of the needs listed on the "How You Will Meet Your Spouse's Needs" page.

d.   After you have completed the list, return it to your spouse and compare the answers on the "How Your Spouse Will Meet Your Needs" to "How You will Meet Your Spouse's Needs." Discuss the differences. Do not be critical of the list your spouse has written. These needs are real to him/her. Talk about why those needs are important to you. Resolve to meet the needs of your spouse. Keep this list. Look at your spouse's list. Refer to it often. Pray. Ask God to help you fulfill these needs for your spouse.

2.   Instead of saying to your spouse, "I Love You," use the phrase "I Need You." Those three words increase the understanding of how much you need your spouse.

3.   Purchase and read the book "His Needs, Her Needs" by Willard Harley. Listed in the book are five needs of a wife and five needs of a husband. A husband or wife knows what their personal needs are. Instead of reading those, read the ones for your mate first. Then discuss with your spouse if those needs are truly what is needed by him/her in your marriage.

4. Determine your mate's weaknesses and strengths to meet the needs in your marriage. Set aside time and give your spouse time to express to you areas in his/her life where they are weak. Ask your spouse what you can do to help them to improve in the area he/she is weakest. Have the same discussion regarding your mate's strengths.

NOTES:

REFLECTING ON EACH OTHER - THE NEEDS OF A WIFE

A. Read 1 Peter 3:1-7. What do you believe your wife needs from you as a husband? _____
_____
_____

Have you ever asked your wife what she needs?_____
If you did ask her, how long ago was it, and what did she say she needed? _____
_____

B. What every husband first NEEDS to know about his wife is to *know her*, live with her in an understanding way, and handle her with care. Is it easy? NO! Is it what God knows you can do? YES! A wife is different from her husband, and a husband needs to understand the difference. God's calling for every husband is to give his wife honor. The differences are not only physical, but psychological and emotional. It is important to know the facts and not resort to hearsay, stereotypes, or guesswork.

C. Since she is different, a husband treats his wife differently. Why? Consider this. A few years ago a magazine conducted a survey of husbands and wives. Sex was a husband's number one leisure activity. Reading was a wife's number one leisure activity. This difference is enough for every husband to know he needs to treat his wife differently.

D. Knowing your wife as *"the weaker vessel"* is not meant for you to have to walk on eggshells. It describes her delicate and well-crafted nature. A good example is viewing your wife as fine china, and not a pot, a paper plate, or pan. She is delicate as china and is to be treated with care. Why? Your wife is more valuable than any other possession you have because she is placed as a gift of God in your life.

Your **wife** is **different** from you, and you need to **understand** the **difference**. **God's calling** for every husband is to **give his wife honor**.

E. Not learning about these differences in his wife, a husband will become frustrated, confused, and sometimes infuriated with her. A husband's unwillingness to know the needs of his wife will lead to these attitudes. Why describe your wife as "touchy," "emotional," "sensitive," "moody," etc.? Listen to her. Watch her. Pay attention to her. Do not try to figure her out. You may think she needs you to work twelve hour days, and have a tough exterior. What she really needs is for you to learn about her, how to live with her, and help her be all God wants her to be.

F. When a husband does not work to know his wife, the results could be like this letter from a wife about her husband: *"I'm afraid I am losing respect for my husband as a man. He is not really contributing to our marriage or even to his own life. It's like having a dependent rather than a husband, a partner."*

The **woman** is a **reflection** of her **husband**. She reflects how she **feels** about her **husband** in her face, attitude, and appearance.

G. A good marriage does not "just happen." A good marriage is two people working together and understanding one another's needs with love and sacrifice daily.

H. What do Romans 15:2,3 and 1 Corinthians 7:33 say about a husband's attitude toward his wife? _____
_____
_____

I. Instead of waking up every day with the thought "I don't know what to do for her." You can replace it with, "I know what is important to her," by understanding her NEEDS. What are they? _____
_____
_____

J. Spiritual Leadership (1 Peter 3:1,2,7).

1. This woman in 1 Peter 3 lacks a relationship with a man on the most intimate level (spiritual). She does not have a deep relationship with the one person who can share God with her—her husband. EX: A wife once said about her husband not fulfilling this need for her, "I need him to come to church with me to help me."

2. A woman needs a relationship with the God who made her. She needs a husband who guides her by His Word so she feels confident about her role before God. Your wife needs you to lead, to love, and to serve spiritually. Many wives ask their husbands, "Do you think I should _____," "I don't

know what to do about _____." She needs to believe in herself and not have doubts and insecurity. Lead her spiritually.

3. Leading her spiritually does not mean quoting scripture, memorizing passages, or preaching a sermon to get his wife to do what he wants. It is understanding what the scriptures say and using them as a guide for loving (not manipulating) your wife. EX: Colossians 3:12,13. Spend the next year focusing on developing those spiritual qualities and make a radical change in how you love your wife.

4. Pray WITH her and FOR her daily, putting your arms around her, and saying, "I want to ask God to bless you. I want to take any needs you have in your life right now to the Lord. I'm going to pray for you throughout this day."

5. The assurance your wife gains, the protection she feels, and the love she experiences because you lead her spiritually are immeasurable. Failing to help fulfill this need in your wife enables her to be the leader in this area.

6. What three things can you do to spiritually lead your wife? Example: 30 Ways to Spiritually Lead Your Wife (See page 128). _____
    _____
    _____

K. Honor Her With Affection 1 Peter 3:7.

1. How do you show affection to your wife? _____
    _____

2. Forms of affection and attention your wife will love: [Hug, kiss, a non-sexual touch, tell her you love her, date her, wash the car, hold her hand, call her, a special term of endearment, short love notes, words of appreciation, flowers, an evening away without children, etc.].

    a. *Praise her with sincerity.* Husbands should tell their wife good things about her, and tell her often. You can never tell her enough how pretty she is.

    b. *Say something about every area of her life.* Do not just concentrate on physical things to affirm her. Compliment her mind, heart, character, motherhood, cooking, etc.

    c. *Never use sarcasm.* Never compliment your wife in a backhanded manner. It damages her spirit. EX: Do not say, "You have a great body—under all that fat!" You think it is cute. She does not.

    d. *If you correct or confront her, compliment her also.* A wife dies emotionally under a barrage of criticism and put-downs. She will become bitter, insecure, and lose trust in her husband.

3. Develop a list of ways you can show affection to your wife. EX: "101 Ways to Love Your Wife" (See page 129). _____
    _____
    _____

4. Certain ways you choose to show affection to your wife may not be easy to develop. Do the easiest acts of affection first, then be creative (breakfast in bed, take her to her favorite coffee shop, etc.) EX: A wife was sanding some chairs on the back porch when her husband came in from work. He went out on the porch to be with her and help her. Things like this motivate a woman to be your woman.

5. Affection for your husband is often for bedtime romance, but it is not for your wife. Affection is what covers your marriage and may lead to sex. A wife needs affection before sex means anything to her. Therefore, a husband must always consider touching his wife's heart before he touches her body. She wants to be emotionally connected to you before being touched sexually. When a man pursues a relationship with his wife and gives her compliments only when he is interested in sex, his wife feels used. This motivates her to withdraw from him.

6. There are several reasons a wife needs affection: she gives birth to a child, has menstrual periods, is at home with children, menopause, and experiences "the empty nest." In all of those times, she needs affection, not blame or criticism.

7. The most honor given to your wife is when you show her affection. Deserving the affection is not the issue; she needs it. Affection from you tells her: "I will take care of you. You are protected. You are important to me. I am concerned about you. I think about you. You do a good job. I am glad to have you in my life." Affection gives your wife security, comfort, approval and it tells her she is being pursued and set apart by her man. This develops—A ONEness RELATIONSHIP. A godly woman responds to this type of husband.

8. The woman is a reflection of her husband. She reflects how she feels about her husband in her face, attitude, and appearance. When a husband creates an atmosphere of praise and respect for his wife, it makes a noticeable difference in everything she does. She radiates and reflects love and respect from every area of her life. It shows.

L. Talk WITH Her Not AT Her - Conversation.

1. What type of conversation is mentioned in Ephesians 4:15, 25, 29? _____
   _____
   _____

2. Most women have a hard time with communication. TRUE or FALSE

3. Most men have a hard time with communication. TRUE or FALSE

4. Philippians 2:2 speaks of having "the same mind, having the same love, being of one accord." How is it possible in marriage without conversation?

5. Yelling, verbal abuse, blaming, complaining, criticism, being defensive, being negative, and being silent produce negative effects in the mental relationship. These are conversation killers.

6. Talking *WITH* your wife, not *TO* her makes for great conversation and intimacy. Not only talking with her, but how you talk with her makes a difference. EX: "I'm going TO tell you what TO do..." "Listen TO me..." "You need TO..." This type of conversation is the marriage of most couples. The more you talk "TO" your wife the greater the chance your tongue will become searing and accusing to her.

7. Some wives often ask, "Why doesn't my husband talk to me anymore?" "I can't get him to talk to me." Why does it have to stop? A growing marriage keeps conversation alive. Not lively like a WWF wrestling match, but lively in warm words and understanding tones.

8. For a wife, the need for conversation means giving her the opportunity to speak. Her expressions in conversation are something a husband should appreciate, not mock and criticize. Every husband appreciated the conversation before being married. You spent hours talking to each other in person or on the phone and had plenty of things to say. The reason you talked so much and so long is (1) you wanted to learn about each other, and (2) you wanted to let the other person know how much you cared.

9. James 1:19 best describes the type conversation a wife needs from her husband. When you sit down and let your wife talk, this is affection. It tells her she has your undivided attention and you value what she has to say. It is through her conversation you can complete what 1 Peter 3:7 says in living with your wife in an understanding way.

10. What obstacles can stand in the way of your conversation with your wife? __
_____

11. What can a husband do to support his wife's need for conversation? _____
_____
_____

12. Conversation takes TIME – your undivided time. Not over or through a TV, computer, or radio.

13. The typical marriage spends four minutes per day on meaningful conversation. If you want to be a romantic man, have regular conversations with your wife, not grunts and one-word answers. Taking time to talk with your wife may require some lifestyle changes (i.e. eating supper without the TV on, cutting off the computer for 30 minutes, walking and talking rather than sitting and staring, quit going out to the shop after supper, but help her wash dishes). If you have to, change the schedule so conversation happens.

14. Talk about what interest her and discuss mutual interests (i.e. politics, cooking, hobbies, children, or spiritual interests). Ask her about the details of her life and fill her in on the details of your life. Most men are reluctant to reveal what most women have no trouble doing—self-revelation. Most men do not want to talk about dreams, hopes, desires, but when you do, you are bonding with the woman of your dreams. You understand her, and you learn how to build your house (Proverbs 24:3,4).

M. Honesty and Openness.

1. John 8:32 says, "You shall know the truth, and the truth shall make you free." Does your wife have access to ALL of your life? Is your wife being held hostage to your secrets and cover-ups?

2. Your wife wants to know your thoughts, feelings, and details of your life. Men often hold their feelings because they don't want to appear out of control. A husband needs to FREE himself by being honest and sharing what is on his heart. It is not meant to minimize her, scare her, or hurt her, but secure her. A wife needs security from her husband in the form of honesty and openness. If a husband does not display honesty in word and action, he undermines his wife's trust and destroys her security.

3. How would you respond to the following questions from your wife?

   a. Do you like this color? _____

   b. How was your day? _____

   c. Can we go to see my parents this weekend? _____

   d. Could you fix the vacuum cleaner? _____

   e. Did you like my casserole? _____

4. Are you a "born liar," "avoid trouble liar," or "protective liar?" Hiding and concealing does not develop a good relationship with your wife. Lying must be put away (Colossians 3:9).

5. What do Proverbs 12:17 and Proverbs 23:23 say that will help you in being honest with your wife? _____
   _____
   _____

6. One of the great avenues of honesty and openness is PRAYER. You are sharing, revealing, and disclosing things to God. God knows who you are and what you need in prayer. Does your wife?

7. Being open with someone about your spouse or marriage invites trouble. Great marriages thrive on honesty and are ruined by dishonesty. Your wife needs it to build trust and compatibility with you. She should know more about you than any other person in the world.

N. Financial Security.

1. Your wife married you for your money. TRUE or FALSE

2. What exhortation do we receive from Ephesians 4:28 and 1 Timothy 5:8? ___
   _____
   _____

3. From 1 Timothy 6:6-10 and Luke 12:15, what concern does God have regarding money and things? How do these passages impact a husband's effort to provide for his wife? _____
_____

4. A husband vows to take care of his wife, financially and from an intruder. God does not call upon the wife to provide for her husband, nor their family and sometimes resents being the one who "carries the family." She desires to know someone cares for her.

5. When providing for their family, husbands need an honorable job. With this job should come wisdom in setting a standard of living equal with what you provide. Most couples, married within 2 to 5 years, set a standard above what they can afford. As a result, the wife "HAS" to find a job just to "make ends meet." She may work for a period of time to help her husband support the family, but God's design for her is not to financially support the family. Working outside the home can be and has led many wives to be frustrated, bitter, and into an emotional affair with another man.

6. Husbands, you and your wife need to learn how to live within your income. Discern between what is "keeping up with others" and what is needed.

   a. Who spends the most money in your marriage? The wife or the husband? Explain your answer. _____
   _____
   _____

   b. If your wife is working to keep the credit card at a minimum, make the car payment, pay for the children's activities, or work for your vacation, there will be no incentive to cut back. The result is a tired, frustrated, unhappy, unfulfilled, and seriously insecure wife.

   c. Money problems in a marriage are not resolved with thinking "she should do her part." It is about your responsibility to do your part so she can do hers—manage the home.

7. Communicate to your wife the desire to provide for her by...

   a. *Praying for God's blessing and direction.* A woman is tremendously comforted to know her husband is praying and seeking God for financial direction and provision whether there is financial pressure or not.

   b. *Aggressively seek the best employment possible.* Keep the door of opportunity open.

   c. *Being a hard and faithful worker.* A wife needs to know her husband is honest, faithful, and hard-working. A lazy husband or one who cannot keep a job does not gain the respect of his wife, resulting in a problem with submission.

d. *Being a wise money manager.* Every husband is valued greatly in the heart of his wife when he is a diligent steward of the blessings God has given him. Living on a budget may be a necessity and the income viewed as "our money." Separate checkbooks lead to separate lives. It is not a sign of a ONEness marriage. If you do not have a budget, make one and make it together. This puts you in control of the money, not the money in control of you. Failure to make a budget often results in the borrower becoming a slave to others (Prov 22:7). Spending more than you make leads to enormous debt. It also means losing the support of your wife.

8. One of the greatest investments you can make in life is your wife's financial security.

9. Financial security for your wife means more than emotional security. TRUE or FALSE.

O. Family Commitment.

1. A husband's first role in commitment is faithfulness to his wife. What is the instruction given to a husband in Proverbs 5:15? _____
   _____

   Your wife needs to feel secure with your faithfulness whether you are present or absent. Communicate to her often your commitment and the person you desire. If your wife feels you are looking at other women or having other problems with unfaithfulness, she will instinctively withdraw from sex to compensate for your problem.

2. A husband's commitment to his wife is only using the "C" word, never the "D" word—divorce.

3. If a husband allows his work, career, education, or hobbies to become more important than his wife and family, his wife becomes resentful and bitter. Let her know you are committed to her and to your family. She will see that commitment by the decisions you make.

4. What is the role of the husband in Proverbs 22:6, Ephesians 6:4 and 1 Thessalonians 2:10,11? _____
   _____
   _____

5. Wives have no problem relating to the value of those verses above. A wife needs a husband to commit to the same. She needs a husband who eats with the family, attends a child's game together, worships together, prays together, does projects together, disciplines together, etc.

   a. Your wife needs a husband involved in the lives of the people in your family. It does take time, but a husband needs to commit to it. Your wife will appreciate your support of what she is doing to make your home what it should be.

b. Do not isolate yourself from your responsibility by saying "She'll take care of the kids." The success of your family is in your hands, not your wife's hands, although your wife is a huge part of how your family is today. The direction your family is going depends on your commitment to that direction. What lesson is there for husbands to learn in the relationship of Eli and his sons (1 Samuel 2:22-25)? _____

_____

_____

6. Your wife needs you to uphold her actions in teaching and correcting your children. Share the parenting responsibilities. Consistent discipline of children is essential to the well-being of a family. It comes from a married couple united with what God wants their children to be.

7. Take care of things at the house (repairs, maintenance, etc.). Fix it if you can, let someone else fix it if you cannot. If a car problem or house problem does not matter to you, your wife will let you know in time, "you don't matter." What does Ecclesiastes 10:18 say can happen from laziness? _____

_____

P. Why Do These NEEDS Matter?

1. They are NEEDS of your wife. She is what matters. Your wife needs to be honored. Handle her with care.

2. Learning what your wife needs and implementing actions to meet those needs is your effort at making your marriage a ONEness marriage.

3. If these needs are not fulfilled by you, they will be searched for and met by someone or something else.

4. Treat her as a fully participating partner of your marriage. She is not a "side kick" but a "fellow-heir" (1 Pet 3:7). When you recognize your wife as a fully participating partner in your life and marriage, you build her esteem. If you exclude her from your life, you devalue her worth as a person and her identity suffers. Without meeting her needs, you send your wife an unmistakably clear signal saying, "I don't need you. I can live my life without you."

5. You may assume you can put this list in the priority which she values most. Do not assume anything. Ask her. Talk to her.

6. Do you believe the needs of your wife now will be the same 5 years from now? Why or why not? _____

_____

_____

7. STORY: Someone interviewed one of Hollywood's biggest male stars, a man known for his prowess with the opposite sex. At one point he was asked, "What makes a great lover?" "Two things," he replied. "First of all, it is a man who can satisfy one woman over a lifetime. Second, it is a man who can be satisfied with one woman for a lifetime."

Q. Image Builders for Your Marriage.

1. What would you do in a case like this? Jay and Julia are married and have three children. She gets a phone call from a guy whom she has known for 8 years. He finds out her number from her parents, calls her, sends her flowers, and she is drawn to him. She has received affection from someone else. Why is she drawn to him? Her husband shows her little or no affection. The only communication they have is "small talk" when he comes home from work each day. They eat super, then he spends an hour or so with the children, and puts them to bed. She goes and reads a book. He watches T.V. Is their marriage in trouble?

2. What would you do in a case like this? My husband Keith has called me almost every low-life name he could think. He's called me "fat" and said I'm "bad in bed." Although it has been almost eight years ago, Keith said these things. I can't forget them. We've been married seventeen years and the T.V. is still more important to him than me. Recently, while staying in a hotel, I purchased a new nightie. When I changed clothes in front of him, his look was one of disgust. Keith didn't have to say a word. The look on his face told me exactly how he felt about me. I feel so rejected physically I can count on one hand in the last two years the times Keith has told me I look nice. He's never at home in the evenings to help me with the children. On weekends, Keith usually finds something other than his family to keep him busy. When I've tried to talk about this, he yells or speaks down to me. I hate living like this. I don't know where to turn for help.

3. Sit down with your wife without interference from children or electronics and ask her these questions. All these questions do not have to be answered in one evening. Let it last through the week if possible.

   a. How can I become the greatest favor in your heart?

   b. What are the three greatest things I can do for you over the next six months?

   c. What are the three greatest concerns that trouble your heart? Pray about them in front of her.

   d. How does our marriage reflect the image of God? If she does not believe it does, ask her, "What can I do to help our marriage reflect the image of God?"

   e. Write your wife a love letter and place it somewhere you know she will find it?

   f. Allow your wife to evaluate how you are doing in fulfilling her basic needs. Make corrections as needed.

   g. What can I do to cause you to feel more loved and cherished?

   h. What can I do to cause you to feel more respected in your ideas and your role as a wife?

    i.   What can I do to assure you that I hear you and understand what is on your heart?

    j.   What can I do to help you feel more secure?

    k.   What can I do to help you feel more confident in our future direction?

    l.   What attribute would you most like for me to develop?

    m. What attribute would you like me to help you develop in yourself?

    n.   What would indicate to you I really desire to be more Christlike?

    o.   What mutual goal would you like to see us accomplish?

4. In the next two weeks, write a list of ten goals you have for your family. Ask your wife to do the same. Get together and compare the list. Compile a five goal list for your family out of those twenty goals.

NOTES:

REFLECTING ON EACH OTHER - THE NEEDS OF A HUSBAND

by Diane Bain

A. Consider the follow questions:

   1. What must a couple do to stay happily married? ___
      _____
      _____

   2. Why do some marriages succeed and some fail? __
      _____
      _____

   3. What would it take for you to be in love again? How can you restore and sustain the feeling of love in your marriage? _____
      _____
      _____

B. Just about everything you and your spouse do affects the love you have for each other. What you do either builds your love for each other, or it destroys your love (1 Corinthians 7:33-34). Each husband and wife needs to be concerned about pleasing their mate.

C. The things that make him feel good and fulfill him are HIS NEEDS. As you understand the needs of your husband and set out to meet those needs, this love will be restored and rekindled, but so much stronger. You will have a ONENESS marriage. Note the agape love of 1 Corinthians 13.

D. Why are these needs not met? Is it due to ignorance or selfishness?

E. Marriage is two servants in love, living to please one another, not self. Communication is necessary to understand these needs. When you accept the differences and seek ways to fulfill his needs, you will see a change in your marriage. Keep these two verses in your heart.

When you **accept** the **differences** and seek ways to **fulfill his needs**, you will see a **change** in your **marriage**.

1 Corinthians 13:5 - Love does not seek its own. Philippians 2:3-4 - Regard him more than yourself.

F. Why should you meet the needs of your husband? _____
_____
_____
_____

G. *The Needs of our Husband* - What are they? Studies have found the following to be the top Six needs causing men the most problems when not met. There are other needs, which your husband may have, but these appear to be top on the list for most men.

1. *Sexual Fulfillment.*

   a. Our sexuality comes from God. He planned and created it. His plan is for us to discover and revel in its mystery and wonder. "*Sex is good because the God who created sex is good. God is glorified greatly when we receive it with thanksgiving and enjoy it the way He meant for it to be enjoyed.*" When we talk about sex the way God designed, we see the beauty, the wonder, and the holiness of this relationship.

   b. Why did God give us the gift?

      1. The ultimate purpose of sex is a celebration of our oneness in the sight of God. Genesis 2:24 says, "they became _____ _____". This "one flesh" experience is a complete expression of body, mind, and spirit, involving a giving and receiving. We become "one flesh" physically, emotionally, and spiritually.

         a. A satisfying sex life is built on a foundation of commitment, companionship, passion, spiritual intimacy.

         b. In Ephesians 5, the marriage relationship is compared to _____ and the _____. A beautiful relationship—One body, One flesh, One person. God takes the most intimate relationship on earth and mirrors it to our spiritual relationship.

         c. The spiritual oneness (spiritual intimacy) you have with your husband will enhance your sexual oneness more

Be a **woman** of **elegance** for your husband. Look **beautiful** in every aspect of your life—your **talk**, your **walk**, your **smile**, and your **demeanor**. Be a **confident** woman.

than you can imagine. Fall in love with God so you can fall in love with your husband.

d. If you are not connected spiritually and emotionally, the sexual connection will not be there either.

2. Pleasure. God created sex to be enjoyable, pleasurable, and passionate in marriage. The Song of Solomon paints a beautiful picture of the sexual union in marriage. It is a story of a man and woman longing for each other, finding each other, and enjoying being together. A celebration of love for both of them. This book can inspire our marriage to be just like them. Read Song of Solomon 2, 5, and 7 and Proverbs 5:15-19.

3. Protection. Avoid temptation. In 1 Corinthians 7:1-5, God knows our desires and gives us the right way to fulfill them.

a. You have the power to protect your husband from temptation by making sure his sexual needs are met by you and you alone. You play a powerful role in helping him not yield to this temptation.

b. When you fail to meet this great need your husband has, it will cause him to be hurt, disappointed, and angry, and lead him to give up on the relationship and seek alternative sexual outlets.

c. Think about the word "DUTY". What does it mean? _____
_____
_____
_____

d. Hebrews 13:4 *"Let marriage be held in honor among all, and let the marriage bed be _____, for fornicators and adulterers God will judge."* What does "undefiled" mean? _____
_____
_____

c. List some things that may hinder romance in your marriage? _____
_____
_____
_____

d. How do I develop this sexual intimacy in my marriage? How can I get back those romantic feelings I once had?

1. Give time and attention to it.

2. Have a plan.

2. *Recreational Companion* - Spend time together having fun.

   a. Do you prefer being with your husband more than anyone else? _____

   b. What are some things you and your husband do together for fun? _____
      _____
      _____
      _____

   c. Many times we slowly drift apart in this area after marriage. He does his thing and you do yours. The more activities done apart, the more opportunity Satan has to separate you.

   d. The tendency is to place the marriage on hold, thinking the time for US will come one day. One day things will calm down. Make the time NOW, because the marriage is worth it.

   e. Find some mutual recreational interest, even if you have to try something new. The more time you spend together, the happier and more fulfilled you will be. Your husband wants you to be with him.

   f. The couple that plays together stays together.

   g. Laugh together. Have fun in your marriage. Be your husband's best friend.

3. *Attractive Spouse*—Your husband needs a good looking wife (in every aspect of life).

   a. Your appearance communicates to your husband his importance in your life.

   b. Think about it...

      1. What first attracts a man to a woman? _____
         _____

      2. What first attracted you to your husband? _____
         _____

   c. Your appearance is probably the first thing drawing him to you. This outward beauty coupled with the valuable inward beauty makes you desireable to him. Proverbs 31:30 says, "*Charm is deceitful and beauty is vain.*"

   d. Your husband appreciates an attractive wife. Be the woman he married many years ago. He fell in love with you, so keep him in love with you. He liked what he saw in you and you want to stay attractive to him.

   e. Recall the story of Ruth. In Ruth 3:3, why was Ruth preparing herself with her best clothes? _____
      _____
      _____

f. Proverbs 31:22, 25 indicates the worthy woman cared about her appearance.

    1. Verse 22 - Her clothing was _____ and _____.

    2. Verse 25 - _____ and _____are her clothing.

g. Be a woman of elegance for your husband. Look beautiful in every aspect of your life—your talk, your walk, your smile, and your demeanor. Be a confident woman.

h. Take care of yourself - your body and your heart. Keep your heart healthy so you grow spiritually. Be attractive on the inside and outside, having a heart of love and compassion.

i. Remember to smile often at your husband because it can soften his heart.

j. Dress modestly. Consider 1 Timothy 2:9-10. Modesty is about preserving the precious gift God has given you for one man.

4. *Domestic Support* - Your husband needs peace and quietness at home.

a. Your husband has many responsibilities. He is to be the head of the home (Ephesians 5:23-24). He is the protector and physical provider (Genesis 3:17-19, I Timothy 5:8). He is the spiritual leader (1 Corinthians 11:3 and Ephesians 6:4).

b. All these responsibilities require a lot of work and are stressful at times. Step into his world, feel the load, and understand what he feels. You may not be able to change the situation, but you can support him as he carries the load.

c. What are some things you can do to make your husband's load a little lighter? _____ _____ _____ Ask your husband often, "What can I do for you today?"

d. Remember, as a wife, you are the keeper of the home (Titus 2:5; I Timothy 5:14; Proverbs 31:27). What does "keeper of the home" mean? _____ _____ _____

e. READ Proverbs 31:27. How does the Worthy Woman give domestic support to her husband? _____ _____

f. Describe meal time at your house? Do you cook good meals for him? The old saying is, "The way to a man's heart is through his stomach." When he comes home from work does he smell good food cooking? Do you eat together at the table with the family? Do you and your husband spend time talking?

g. Be thankful and take care of your home. No matter what kind of house you have.

1. Tell your husband how much you appreciate your home and what he provides for you.

2. Make your home a place he longs to be with you, away from the stresses of the world.

3. Your home is your refuge - a place of peace and order - a place he can renew himself in body and spirit. When he is driving home from work, is he looking forward to getting there to see you or is he dreading what he will meet at the door? You want him to want to come home.

h. Be thrifty with what you have. Providing this need for your husband takes planning, work, and being organized.

5. *Admiration* - Two powerful tools used by a wife to influence her husband are respect and admiration.

a. Admiration helps your husband believe in himself and energizes him. Your husband expects you to be his most enthusiastic fan. He draws confidence from your support and achieves far more with your encouragement.

b. Appreciate and respect your husband for who he is, not for what he could become if he lived up to your standards.

c. He is the man you married; accept him and love him for who is he apart from his performance.

d. You have heard it said, "Behind every good man is a good woman cheering him on." Every husband needs a wife who believes in him, appreciates him, and encourages him as he goes out into the world every day.

e. The word *appreciate* means to raise in value. Proverbs 31:12 says, "She does him good all the days of her life." Through your words of admiration, you help him become the man God intends for him to be.

f. A woman is like a motor in a car - essential for the car to run, but it is not seen, because it is under the hood. Support and encourage your husband as he pursues his dreams. Do whatever you can to help him and celebrate his accomplishments with him. Ask your husband, "What can I do to help you accomplish your goals, dreams?"

g. Proverbs 18:21 says, "Death and life are in the power of the tongue." Your words can bring hope and encouragement to your husband or they can bring doubt and discouragement. You build him up or tear him down by your words.

h. List some ways you can show admiration to your husband. _____
    _____
    _____

i. Be thankful for your husband and all he does for you and the family; telling
    him often. Compliment him in front of others.

j. The greatest fear for most men is failure and their deepest need is con-
    fidence to know they can succeed. Men are drawn to people who honor
    and respect them. Let him be drawn to you.

k. When your husband fails, loses a job, doesn't get the raise, etc., do not
    leave him alone to deal with his disappointments. Tell him your love is
    consistent and pray for him. Encourage him to keep going and trust in
    God for strength. It only takes a few seconds to give your husband a word
    of praise, but it could make a big difference in his life. Believe in him even
    when he does not believe in himself.

l. Be quick to forgive your husband when his error has affected you. The
    act of forgiveness opens the door to healing, allowing you to move on in
    your marriage. When your husband makes mistakes, give him grace, just
    as God does with you when you make mistakes.

    1. Remember Ephesians 4:32. "Be kind one to another, forgiving one
        another".

    2. Colossians 3:12-13 says, "Put on a heart of compassion, kindness,
        humility...bearing one another, and forgiving one another..."

    3. James 5:16 - " _____ your faults to one another..." Can you
        confess your faults to your husband?

6. *Communication.*

    a. Communication in a marriage builds your relationship or tears it down.
        Our words are like seeds. Once planted in your husband, they bring forth
        flowers or weeds, health or disease, healing or poison.

    b. In "The Five Love Languages," Gary Chapman identifies ways we can
        communicate to each other—Touch - Gifts - Acts of Service - Words of
        Admiration - Time.

    c. When you communicate with your husband, you must be open and honest.
        There is no room for privacy in marriage (2 Timothy 1:7).

    d. Communication takes TIME and being too busy inhibits opportunities to
        communicate.

        1. Listen to your husband (James 1:19). Show interest. Stop and look
            at him.

       2.   Communicate to understand him (Proverbs 22:17). Ask questions to clarify what he is saying rather than arguing with him.

       3.   Let him talk (Proverbs 10:19). Be wise!

       4.   Set aside some time each day to talk to each other. You may have to adjust your schedule to make this happen. Be on the same clock.

       5.   Plan a yearly getaway together. Spend time talking, sharing, planning, reflecting, and dreaming.

  e. Proverbs 15:1 speaks of a gentle answer. What you say, how you say it, your attitude, your honesty, your attentiveness, your understanding, your time, and your touch ALL make a difference in communication.

  f. Choose your words carefully. Ask yourself, "Is what I am about to say disrespectful?"

  g. Sometimes it is not the words you say, it is how you say them. You communicate by the tone of voice, facial expressions, and word selection. Do you have a sour, dark look, and a scolding finger pointed? If you treat your husband with respect, he will listen to you.

  h. Pray daily for your husband. Be specific.

       1.   Pray for yourself. God will help you be the helpmeet, the companion, the lover, the support, and the encouragement to him. Prayer changes your attitude about yourself and your husband.

       2.   Remember...

           a.   Colossians 1:9-11 - We must be strengthened with the power of His might. God will help you be this kind of wife.

           b.   Psalms 18:1-3 - God is my strength.

           c.   Philippians 4:13 - "I can do all things through Christ that strengthens me."

H. Love is something you do for someone else, NOT something you do for yourself. You meet HIS NEEDS for his benefit. When you give your husband what he NEEDS, you get what you need.

I. Work daily to meet the needs of your husband. He will be the happy man you want when he feels you accept him as he is, admire him, and put him first (after God) in your life. He will feel needed at home because he knows he is respected as the family leader, provider, and protector.

J. As you respond to your husband in meeting his needs, you will see great things happening in your marriage. Your husband will feel complete and fulfilled. Marriage is much like a garden. It takes work, constant attention, and time to grow. If you neglect it, it will be overtaken by the world. Pay attention and invest your life to be the wife God wants you to be. You will be blessed.

NOTES:

REFLECTING UPON MY ROLE - LEADERSHIP OF A HUSBAND & SUBMISSION OF A WIFE

by Diane Bain

Leadership Of A Husband
by Sean Bain

A. The leadership qualities of a husband are found in Ephesians 5:23-31.

   1. Every man has the underlying expectation of being the "head" (v.23). The real question is what kind of head.

   2. As the head, every husband is to lead his wife like Jesus, "as Christ also is...head...loved...nourisheth and cherisheth..." (vv. 23, 25, 29).

B. What kind of husband should a wife have?

   1. Leader (v. 23) - Spiritually and physically.

   2. Dedicated (v. 25) - Sacrificial, promoting purity, keeping their union sanctified.

   3. Gentle (v. 28) - No harm to himself or his wife.

   4. Devoted (v. 29) - He is committed to his vows, to leaving his family for his wife, affectionate, dedicated to his wife.

   5. Faithful (v. 31) - A man who wants to be married for life and knows the ups and downs of marriage handles them with the view "we will make it through this."

C. You should already be this man, if not, you need to be.

D. What Does Leadership In Marriage Mean?

   1. *Accepting the Role.*

> If the **husband** does **not lead**, the **woman** will. If **she does**, a **husband** will **complain** about what she does.

    a. Consider the first person God approached in the garden after the sin? "... *she gave...he ate,*" (Gen 3:6). God comes to Adam. Adam needed to have listened to God's voice rather than her voice.

    b. If the husband does not lead, the woman will. If she does, a husband will complain about what she does.

    c. Leadership in marriage is not about who is the better leader. It is about function – where God placed the husband.

    d. The seriousness of leadership in marriage is found in 1 Timothy 3:5.

2. *Learn to Judge in Righteousness.*

    a. Abraham. Describe the leadership of Abraham in Genesis 18:19? _____
    _____

    b. As a husband, let your judgment be characterized by righteousness and the fear of God.

    c. Judgment in righteousness is God's way for you to *PROTECT* your marriage.

        1. Protect your marriage from immoral things, poverty, and false teaching.

        2. Protect your marriage by being a spiritual leader.

            a. Noah (Genesis 6:8; Hebrews 11:7).

            b. Understand and pray for your wife (1 Peter 3:7).

        3. In 2 Timothy 1:7 what is the Spirit with which you can protect your marriage? _____
        _____

        4. In Ephesians 4:14 what principle can a husband have to protect his marriage? _____
        _____

    d. If you are looking for respect from your wife, then learn to judge with discretion.

3. *Have a Vision.*

    a. Without vision, your marriage will perish (Proverbs 29:18).

    b. The vision for your marriage is found in Ephesians 5:22-33.

    c. What is the vision you have for your wife? _____
    _____

4. *Let God do His work in you.*

    a. Be the right person to the woman you chose. Do not surrender yourself to domination.

    b. Know what a husband is to be by first talking to God and letting God talk to you. Do not surrender to chance.

    c. Do not surrender your love for your wife to the admiration of another.

    d. Do not surrender to things in life breaking your marriage (i.e. money, job, hobbies, positions).

    e. Surrender to Jesus and become an irresistible man when you lead your wife by following God, not the world (Mark 8:34-38).

NOTES:

Submission Of A Wife   by Diane Bain

A. Being in submission to your husband is God's plan for the wife.

B. Notice the following passages.

1. Genesis 3:16 - The husband will rule over you.

2. Ephesians 5:22-24,33 - Wives, be in subjection. Respect your husband.

3. Colossians 3:18 - Be in subjection.

4. Titus 2:3-4 - Teach younger women to be in submission.

5. 1 Peter 3:1-5 - Submissive. The husband may be won to the Lord by a wife's behavior.

C. Before a wife can be in submission to her husband, she must be in submission to God. You must yield to His will. When you have not surrendered to God and His authority, then you do not trust God to work in your life. This is where a wife struggles.

D. When you surrender to God and accept His will, then being in submission to your husband will not be an issue in your life. It will become your way of life. Being obedient to your husband is part of your obedience to Christ.

E. God knew from the beginning of time that there had to be organization in life. There had to be rules and people in authority. If not, things would be chaos. So, whether male or female, single or married, we are required to submit to God (James 4:7), to the elders of the church (Hebrews 13:17), to our employers (1 Peter 2:18), and to the government (1 Peter 2:13-14). In the marriage relationship, the wife is to submit to her husband.

F. What does being in submission mean? _____
_____

1. Being a submissive wife means yielding to the power and authority of your husband. It is voluntarily cooperating with your husband, being under his authority, and letting him lead.

2. Submission is respecting your husband and supporting him in what he does when it is in accordance to God's will. You are the responder to his love, protection, and leadership. Your husband leads and you respond to that lead.

3. Submission is something the wife gives, not something a husband demands. Jesus did not forcefully hold to equality with God. He voluntary submitted.

G. The Bible says God's ways are not our ways. His thoughts are not our thoughts. Submission is contrary to the way you think in your human reasoning. Yet, God has a purpose in submission far beyond us. When you are willing to submit to God by giving up your rights and submitting to your husband, you will experience a peace and joy not found in other ways. Your life could be simplified if you go back to the scriptures and listen to God's way. Trust God's plan for you.

H. What are some reasons wives do not submit to their husbands? _____
_____
_____
_____

I. When you submit to your husband, you allow him to be the man God intended for him to be. It frees him to be the leader and builds his confidence.

J. Submission has a lot to do with the attitude with which you approach your husband. Your gentleness, your meek and quiet spirit, and your respect show a submissive attitude (1 Peter 3:4). It is an attitude important to God and indicates your willingness to align yourself with your husband and follow. You are yielding to his wishes.

K. Respect is the important factor in submission. Respect is something you give because it is the right thing to do. Remember Ephesians 5:33 speaks of the importance of respecting your husband.

   1. How can you show respect to your husband? _____
   _____
   _____

   2. Remember this: The more submissive a wife becomes, the more likely her husband will be open to her suggestions. Be submissive, kind, and gentle, so your husband will respond.

   3. When your husband sees your effort to honor his role by showing respect and adapting yourself to him, he is motivated to please you too. He will ask for your input. Consider the principle of Luke 6:38.

   4. Ephesians 5:25-29. Your husband sacrifices his wants and needs to please and build up his wife.

L. Your husband needs to fulfill the design God has for him and to be all God wants him to be. A husband tries to lead his wife and family, but at times the wife rules over him and gets her way. After a while, the dominated husband will quit leading, shut down, and isolate himself from you. Wanting peace in the home more than leadership, he quits leading and lets his wife have her way. Shame on the woman who does this. When you do

Before a **wife** can be in **submission** to her **husband,** she **must** be in **submission** to **God**. You must **yield to His will** for you.

this, you are showing disrespect to your husband and to God. This is not God's plan for you.

M. When a husband leads, he is submitting to Christ. In Ephesians 5:25, the husband is to yield to God by loving his wife as _____ loved the _____; in Ephesians 5:22 by being the final decision maker; in Ephesians 5:26 by being the spiritual head; and in 1 Peter 3:7 by living with her in an understanding way.

N. The husband/wife relationship is an earthly picture of the relationship between Christ and the church. Just as the church is totally dependent on Jesus Christ, so the wife is totally dependent on her husband. As you show reverence to your husband, you are creating a picture of how the church shows reverence to Christ. In this atmosphere, you are protected and fulfilled and your husband is inspired to be the man God created him to be.

O. Think about this! With Christ being head over man, what did Jesus do? He gave His life to meet the needs of man's soul. As the head, your husband is to use his leadership to please, meet the needs, and serve you. Your husband is looking out for your best interest.

P. Your husband leads in many different ways.
Think about the spiritual leading he does for his family in the ways of God. How can you support your husband in his desire to lead your family spiritually? _____
_____
_____

Ask your husband, "What can I do to help you feel more loved, respected, and supported in our marriage?"

Q. What to do when there is a disagreement?

1. The first thing you should do is STOP. Take time to collect your thoughts and keep yourself from reacting emotionally and saying or doing something foolish.

2. Pray for the right kind of spirit.

3. Speak the truth in Love. The key is "in love." Share your thoughts with your husband in love, not in frustration and anger. When you share the truth in love, you will speak honestly, with the right tone of voice, facial expression, and gestures.

4. If your husband still does not agree with you, submit (yield) to his wishes and give this issue to God. Husbands have the responsibility and accountability to God to lead the family in the right way. Trust him to do it.

5. Submission is such a powerful principle because it operates on faith, and without faith it is impossible to please God (Hebrews 11:6). It takes faith to believe God will intervene on our behalf.

6. Patience is key. Patience is one of the main ingredients necessary for success-fully submitting in life. Yet, it is sorely lacking in most of our lives, because it requires us to release control of a situation. We must walk in faith, believe

God will intervene when we are called to submit to someone in authority. Sometimes submission means waiting patiently for your husband to make a decision.

7. When the situation is released into the Lord's hands, you will experience peace even before the situation is resolved. One man wrote about his wife's submission to him: *"I remember the day my wife turned me over to the Lord. She didn't tell me that's what she had done, but I knew it had taken place. Before, when she would contend with me, it allowed me to justify decisions I knew were not pleasing to the Lord. But when she relinquished control, the only person I had to deal with was the Lord and that's an uncomfortable position."*

R. Submission has nothing to do with your husband being a believer or non-believer. In 1 Peter 3:1-5, living your commitment to God can win your husband to Christ. Submission is a strong point here for a wife. Through your submission and your meek and quiet spirit, you can teach your husband the value of giving up his will for Christ.

1. This can be very difficult, but with God's help you can be this kind of woman.

2. In 1 Peter 3:8-17, this kind of spirit or attitude is to be desired and it is what God wants. There are times when you are unhappy, have to suffer, or think he doesn't deserve your respect. Satan will encourage you to leave, give up, render evil for evil, be disrespectful, withhold yourself from him, and isolate yourself.

3. In verse 14, "...even if you should suffer for the sake of righteousness, you will be blessed."

4. Verse 17, "...it is better if God should will it so, that you suffer for doing right rather than for doing what is wrong."

5. Unholy behavior cannot be used to achieve holy behavior. Showing disrespect toward him will not change him.

6. It is not about him earning your respect, you respect him for who he is apart from his performance. The only exception would be when your husband's specific demands go against God's word. Colossians 3:18 says, "as it is fit in the Lord".

S. Submission brings glory to God, avoids problems in the home, encourages your husband in growth and maturity, builds respect and honor to your husband, and portrays Christ and the church (Ephesians 5).

T. Your marriage is happy because of the choices you make every day. Pray to God and ask him to help you be the right helpmeet for your husband.

U. Image Builders for Your Marriage.

1. Pray about this. Ask God to give you this kind of spirit. Pray for your husband to lead you. Tell him you need his leadership. Let him lead. When he does lead you, praise him and thank him.

2. Can I do these things? Yes, Philippians 4:13.

3. Must I do these things? Yes, Titus 2:4-5.

4. Will I do these things? You have to answer this question.

NOTES:

FOCUSED MARRIAGE IN A BUSY WORLD

A. Read Ezra 1. What was the decree of Cyrus, king of Persia? _____

B. Can you imagine how anxious the people of God were to get back to their homeland and begin the process of rebuilding the house of God? The appointments were given and the work started (Ezra 3). This good work of rebuilding the temple was frustrated by Judah's enemies (Ezra 4). They were criticized before King Artaxerxes and accused of building "the rebellious and bad city" (Ezra 4:12). By decree and force, Judah ceased building the house of God. What does Haggai 1:1-11 describe as the reason Judah had ceased from building the house of God? _____
_____
_____

C. As priorities shifted, their efforts were frustrated and the enemies pressed against them. Judah stopped building God's house to build their own houses. In similar fashion, many couples have become frustrated and are floundering in their marriage. At one time, these couples were building a great marriage. Disrespect, criticism, communication problems, and infidelity have replaced the joy, oneness, and attention their marriage once had. Some will say, "We've grown apart. We don't have anything in common". Translated, it means they are not spending enough time alone, "together." Therefore, one of the most important lessons for your marriage is TIME.

D. Before marriage, you could not get enough of each other. While you were dating, you "made time" for each other. You made time for each other in the midst of work, school, homework, dentist and dermatology appointments, ballgames, piano, karate, and football practices.

Busyness has caused many couples to **grow apart** after ten, twenty, or thirty years of marriage. **Couples** are **caught** in a vortex and cannot seem to find **a way out**.

What steals time away from many **marriages** is the **lack of knowledge. Couples** do **not know** "how to do marriage".

E. Being married, the responsibilities increased and our connection with each other decreased. Some marriages cannot relax. They start, but never finish. They have no boundaries. They cannot get out of the storm. They are overachievers. They are competitors. They cannot enjoy quiet. Busyness has caused many couples to grow apart after ten, twenty, or thirty years of marriage. Couples are caught in a vortex and cannot find a way out. What will be the outcome of your marriage? Will you spend the rest of our marriage in isolation and independence, or will you "redeem the time"?

F. You must understand that your relationship as husband and wife is the foundation of your family. If it fails, everything fails. When a married couple complains, "We can't seem to find the time," it is often associated with some other problems like his lack of affection, her lack of sex, his anger, her lack of appreciation, etc. Is your marriage really suffering from being "time-starved"?

G. What Is Snatching Your TIME?

1. What are some of the time bandits in your marriage? _____
_____
_____

2. Are these time bandits planned, or unpredictable?
_____

3. Unfinished business, busyness, technology, impatience, overcommitment, and misplaced priorities are a few of the things most married couples have allowed in their marriage. These things are disturbing our life and our married life. They have undermined any effort to make your marriage a reflection of the image of God.

4. Most couples say busyness is the number one thief of time in their marriage. Is there a "good busy" (church work, hobbies, sewing, etc.) and "bad busy" (frazzled, lazy, wasting time)? Can busyness be placed in one category or another or does it all meld together? _____
_____

5. Busyness is like a corrosive agent. It takes away the things we really want in the relationship and zaps our energy. When you lose your sense of humor, you know life is too busy. You get short with each

other, taking the fun out of marriage. You get task oriented, losing affection for one another.

6. What instruction does Ephesians 5:15-17 give in relation to time? How should the principles of that passage affect your marriage? _____
   _____
   _____

7. In marriage, what biblical term do you believe best describes the value of "being connected" as husband and wife? (EX: fellowship, communion) _____
   _____

   Growth and unity in the church depends upon time spent together (i.e. Acts 2:45,46), so we need the same in our marriage.

8. The lack of knowledge steals time away from many marriages. Couples do not know "how to do marriage." Many couples do not have, as a reference for their marriage, a good example from their own parents. They may pledge a lifelong commitment to one another, but soon begin to repeat the failings of their parents.

9. Greed. The want for more becomes a top priority for many couples.

   a. Greed comes in the form of money.

   b. Greed comes in the form of career engagement, being lost in their skill and expertise.

   c. Greed comes in the form of popularity. The more I make or have, the more others know me.

   d. Greed comes in the form of success. Achievement to excel others is the "big picture."

   e. Greed is the lust for something beyond what we have or need. All the while a couple is sacrificing God and their marriage. More is never enough.

   f. What does Ecclesiastes 2:10, 11, 17, 18 and 4:4-8 teach that would help your marriage? _____
   _____
   _____

   g. What does striving for the "gold ring" do for your marriage? Does success hug you close at night? Will popularity with others make you popular at home? Does position at work mean the position in your marriage is being fulfilled? Remember 1 Timothy 6:10 and Hebrews 13:4,5.

10. Self-gratification. There is a sense of pride that comes when sacrificing for others as a counselor, elder, deacon, teacher, doctor, coach, boss, civic club president, etc. The places where you help, heal, comfort, encourage, lead, etc. are a "lift" to your life, but may isolate you from the one you need to lift - your mate. Seeking a godly work and neglecting your marriage is the wrong goal.

God never said abandon your marriage in order to serve others (1 Timothy 5:8). If service is your goal, serve your marriage and family by placing them as the priority.

11. Willard Harley in his book "His Needs, Her Needs" says a couple needs to spend 15 hours a week in communication. On average a couple spends 1 hour a week with each other communicating. However, a couple in an affair will spend 15 hours a week with each other in spite of the other commitments with current marriage, family, work, etc. Spend at least 8 hours a week with your spouse. You did when you were dating, so why stop when you are married. If your thoughts about your marriage are "we have just grown apart," this means you are not spending time together. If there is no connection, you will feel you are married to a stranger. There is no way you will work on love, affection, money issues, and your relationship. You need *time* together ALONE.

H. Spirituality: The First Casualty of Busyness.

1. What does 1 Corinthians 15:58 and Galatians 6:9 say to your marriage? ____
    _____
    _____

2. Spirituality of marriage is lost due to lack of time. Couples give their time to everything else they believe their marriage needs, but neglect what provides their relationship with strength, stability, and endurance—their spiritual intimacy.

3. What is the spiritual responsibility of a husband in Ephesians 5:25-28? ____
    _____
    _____

4. What is the spiritual responsibility of a wife in 1 Peter 3:1-5? _____
    _____
    _____

5. You choose to give your marriage the spiritual intimacy it needs. If it is not given the time needed, your marriage is at risk and you settle for a marriage less than what God wants or what you hope to have.

6. When priorities are misplaced or shifted around, couples may give attention to others and other things more than their spouse. What would Ecclesiastes 12:13 and Matthew 6:33 say to your marriage? _____
    _____

7. Does a marriage with children and both spouses working have less time or more time for their marriage than a couple with children and only the husband working outside the home? Explain your answer. _____
    _____
    _____

I. What Do We Do To Have a Focused Marriage?

1. How do we remove the thoughts: "My spouse doesn't hear or understand me," "Who cares? Why try?," "I can't please her," "He is so not here," "She is 'checked-out'," "We're doing our own thing."

2. If your barrier is *spiritual exhaustion*, make a schedule of when and how you will work on your spiritual life together. Turn off the TV. Turn off the phone. Close the computer. Put a note on the door. Reserve the time and you will experience a closeness that is priceless.

3. If your barrier is *misplaced priorities*, simply rearrange things. It may mean quitting the PTA or finding another job. It will be worth it for the time your marriage needs.

4. *Pursue God first.* When trouble strikes, it is natural to focus on solving the problem or the person. Plant your attention and focus upon Jesus Christ. Make choices for your marriage which allow you to grow in Him. As a result, you will grow in your marriage. Matthew 6:33 says it all.

5. *Nurture ONENESS* in marriage by listening to Proverbs 24:3,4.

    a. Have Knowledge. Know your responsibilities, not your mate's responsibilities. Know about your mate, then know what you need to do to change you, not your mate. Refuse to find yourself paying more attention to what changes your spouse needs to make.

    b. Yield to Undertanding. Embrace the difference in each other (1 Peter 3:7). Look at those differences through the eyes of God. In order to understand, you need time to communicate.

    c. Adopt Wisdom. James 1:5 exhorts us to pray for wisdom. Take what you know and understand, then act properly and in honor toward your spouse. Wisdom is having a teachable spirit, which is being one who wants to learn how to make their marriage better.

6. *Commit* to the time and work your marriage needs. When you do, a wonderful thing happens. You fall in love with your spouse all over again. Are you scared of that? You should not be. You were not scared before you married. Why be scared now? Your children benefit from your stronger relationship. Your marriage is the foundation upon which your entire family is structured. Children need security in a Dad and Mom who love each other. Your children will never suffer neglect because you make a strong commitment to your spouse. Based upon the attention you are currently giving your marriage, would your children say you believe in marriage?

7. TIME in marriage means...

    a. T – Together.

    b. I - Interest in your spouse.

    c. M – Make it and manage to find time.

    d. E - Eliminate distractions and hurry.

J. Image Builders for Your Marriage.

1. Recall a memorable moment in your marriage. Relive the moment, if it can be replicated.

2. If you had a "moment" with your spouse, what would you reflect upon, say, or do?

3. *Look at the GOOD, not the BAD.* Do not always look at the dirt, what is broken, what is forgotten, or how it was not done right. You married your spouse for a lot of "good reasons". Therefore, look at the GOOD in your spouse and compliment it with thanks (Philippians 4:8 - It is where your thoughts are that count). Ignore the small, little things (i.e. dirty socks on the floor, a day-old coffee cup on the counter, worn out flannel pajamas, an inappropriate burp at the dinner table). Look at the things which make you smile: the way he rolls on the floor with the baby, she made your favorite cookies, and the peace in knowing someone so well you can wear your worn out flannels.

4. Give at least two compliments per day (Ephesians 4:29; 1 Thessalonians 5:18). When you see something you favor, express your joy in what your mate has done. If you say to your spouse, "You're the best," then let them know at what they are the best (i.e. cooking, helping, giving, cleaning).

5. Touch those you compliment (1 Thessalonians 5:21 – "hold fast that which is good"). Hugging and holding your spouse was not the idea in this scripture, but the principle is true. Hold, hug, kiss, rub shoulders, cuddle, etc. the one who exhibits the good. Have a 60 second non-sexual cuddle. Your marriage never ages when it comes to touch. Make your touch with your spouse different and more frequent than a touch, hug, or kiss from your children.

6. Focus on your mate for at least 10 minutes a day, like a 10-minute workout - after supper, before bedtime, before leaving each other for the day. You will see the difference it will make in your marriage. A strong marriage is not obtained automatically or by luck. It takes a daily workout. Give your marriage focused attention for 10 minutes each day and in the next thirty days you will have a better, different marriage.

7. Check the pressure on your marriage. Your marriage needs the "pressure" check to determine if there is too much being allowed into your marriage, hence damaging your relationship with your spouse. Locate the "Check the

Pressure on Your Marriage" (page 71). Answer the questions, then evaluate your results at the end. Share your answers with your spouse.

8. Plan a getaway at least twice a year. Three would be great. Plan it or it will not happen.

9. Allow the words of Galatians 5:13 to permeate your hearts. Be servants one of another in love.

10. Be prepared for attacks on your efforts to focus on building your marriage. In a culture valuing individualism and self-satisfaction, efforts to exemplify godly stewardship, humility, and grace in marriage will be mocked - sometimes from your own family. Withstand negative influences.

11. Pray together. Become spiritually intimate. Husbands read a book about being a better husband. Wives read a book about being a better wife. Couples read a book about marriage. Give your marriage the attention it needs to reflect the image of God - a marriage you will rejoice to have.

NOTES:

CHECK THE PRESSURE ON YOUR MARRIAGE

A. Circle your answer.

1. At the end of the month, our finances are:
    a. Okay, with a little left over.
    b. Tight.
    c. It's a challenge every month and I feel pressure to make ends meet.
    d. Strained to the breaking point—in big trouble soon if something doesn't change.
    e. Melting down. We are about to sink.

2. Our children's schedules are:
    a. Light.
    b. Full, but we're staying on top of it as a couple.
    c. Hectic. At times I feel like their schedules are controlling us.
    d. Out of control. Our lives REVOLVE around their schedules. It's been this way far too long and there's no end in sight.

3. Expectations in our marriage are:
    a. Generally met or exceeded. I'm pretty satisfied.
    b. Some are met and some are not. I can tell there's a little pressure because of it.
    c. There are many unmet expectations and I'm feeling the pressure something must change—and soon.
    d. I don't know what the expectations are.
    e. I've replaced my expectations with resentment toward my spouse. I feel ripped off in this relationship.

4. How is communication in your marriage?
    a. It's not a major problem.
    b. We need a little help here and there.
    c. We have major communication problems and it's causing a lot of pressure.
    d. What communication? We stopped meaningful communication a long time ago. Why try?

5. How do you handle conflict in your marriage?
    a. We pretty much resolve our conflicts as they occur.
    b. We allow the "sun to go down" on our anger about half the time.
    c. We don't resolve conflict well at all. I'm a peacemaker and my spouse is a prizefighter.
    d. We are embittered toward one another.

6. The health of the members of our family is:
   a. Generally fine. Just the usual runny noses, scrapes, and bruises.
   b. Mostly good with an occasional sick child or parent.
   c. Not so good. Chronic pain or illness afflicts one or more of us.
   d. Awful. I've never known a time when we were not dealing with pressure from some health-related issue.

7. When I'm with my spouse:
   a. We use words of affirmation or praise with each other. Sometimes we linger over breakfast or dinner and work hard to connect with one another.
   b. My spouse tends to read the paper, watch TV, or engage in some distraction like doing the dishes while I'm trying to express myself.
   c. Our conversation is abrupt and devoid of genuine love or care. We're polite, but all business.
   d. We lash out at each other more and more. I get steamed over something that has been said at least once a day.

8. The past has:
   a. No grip on either of us.
   b. Occasionally causes my spouse or me tension.
   c. Haunts me and/or my spouse.
   d. Paralyzes us with stress and keeps us from moving forward in our marriage.

9. When I'm at home with my family:
   a. Game playing, laughter, and hugs punctuate the normal ups and downs of life. Our home is a welcoming place.
   b. Sometimes I wish my spouse would demonstrate a greater interest in the children and me.
   c. Yelling, slamming doors, or cold silence is normal. Our home is becoming more like a motel filled with familiar strangers.
   d. Most of the time, I try to be somewhere else.

10. When it comes to divorce:
    a. We've never used the word with each other. I know it's not an option, nor would I ever agree to one.
    b. It's crossed my mind once or twice.
    c. The pressures in our marriage bring divorce to mind more and more of late.
    d. I can't take the pressure in this relationship. I'd get divorced if it weren't for the kids. My best friend is urging me to walk away from it all.

11. Are aging parents adding stress to your marriage?
    a. Our parents are either gone or are doing well on their own. They don't take much of our time.
    b. Our parents are increasing in their dependency upon us. We feel responsible for their well-being at least some of the time.
    c. We are caring for one or more parents regularly.
    d. One or more parents live with us and we are responsible for their care. Frankly, it's weighing heavily upon us.

12. Our house:
    a. Isn't perfect, but we like it and can afford it. We have it decorated more/less the way we want.
    b. We're kind of stretched to make the payments. It doesn't leave much for extras like curtains, paint, or furnishings.
    c. Is too small. I'm stressed out all the time because there's nowhere to put stuff and the kids need their own bedrooms.
    d. Is falling apart. We're in constant repair mode. I hate where we live. The neighborhood isn't safe anymore. I wish we could move.

13. My in-laws:
    a. Are really nice people. They're helpful and a good influence on our kids. What's more, they don't pressure us to visit or do things with them.
    b. Are great if we don't spend too much time together. But we are increasingly feeling the tug and pull to be with them more often.
    c. Sometimes make me uncomfortable when they put their noses in our business. They pressure me to do things, like raising our children, their way.
    d. Never leave us alone. It's as if they're monitoring our lives on video cameras, watching our every move. We're stifled. I can't take the pressure from them anymore.

14. Our children:
    a. Are a joy to have around. We have lots of laughs together and function well as a helping, encouraging family.
    b. Are pretty good kids. They seem to have an upbeat attitude. They're involved in school activities and have good grades.
    c. Tend to be withdrawn, and even secretive. I wish I knew how to connect with their world.
    d. Are disturbed. They've made it clear they hate us. Sometimes I'm afraid of the hostility I see in their eyes. We're feeling the pressure of what to do about it.

15. As a couple we:
    a. Pray often, even daily, and sometimes work on a Bible study together.
    b. Pray at meals, holidays, or when a crisis comes.
    c. Don't talk about the Lord much outside of church. Even then the conversation quickly turns to safer topics. We almost never pray together.
    d. Clash. My spouse is not saved and sometimes disparages my faith.

16. How is your love life?
    a. We enjoy a healthy, romantic relationship with a few adjustments along the way.
    b. We have to work at this area, but we're generally meeting one another's needs.
    c. This area isn't working. The bedroom has become a pressure-filled battleground.
    d. We've both lost hope that we'll ever have a normal sex life together.

17. Are either of you moody?
    a. My spouse and I are both even tempered and easygoing.
    b. There is an occasional mood swing by one or both of us that can result in some uneasy moments.
    c. There is a lot of pressure created by different moods in our marriage and family life.
    d. Mood swings are a way of life and keep things in a constant state of disruption.

18. Do you share the same parenting values?
    a. We're in synch on most child-raising issues.
    b. We occasionally have a sharp disagreement on how to discipline our children.
    c. We continually struggle with our differing values on how to raise the children.
    d. Values? We're from different galaxies.

19. The role of being a spouse is:
    a. Not all that difficult. We both had good role models and know what's expected of each other.
    b. Creating tension in me. Both of us have a fuzzy and incomplete picture of what it means to be a wife and husband.
    c. Upside down. We've flip-flopped our roles and it's causing an enormous amount of pressure in our lives.
    d. Causing major problems. One or both of us is clue-less about the respon-sibilities that come with being a husband or wife.

B. Add your score by totaling the numbers circled. For example, if you circled the third response in a given question, add three points for that answer. If the circle was number one, add one point to your total. The lowest possible score is 20, the highest is 80.

C. In general terms, and based upon what is witnessed in the lives of thousands of couples, here's what your score is telling you about the level of pressure in your marriage and home life:

1. If your score is between 20 and 34, give thanks. This is about as good as it gets.
2. If your score is between 35 and 49, begin tackling the pressure points while there's time.
3. If your score is between 50 and 64, this is your wake-up call. You're close to the edge.
4. If your score is between 65 and 80, seek professional counseling immediately.

THE IMAGE OF COMMUNICATION— HE SAID, SHE SAID

A. "What do I say?" "What do we talk about?" "How can I get him/her to talk to me?" "Why doesn't he/she talk to me anymore?" "All she does is nag?" "He doesn't hear a thing I say!" "I can't believe anything he says!" "She exaggerates all the time." "Why can't she just come out and say what she means?" "Let me tell you what to do!"

B. Have any of the questions or statements above ever been yours? Is there a way a husband and wife can communicate so their marriage will reflect the image of God? Communication is the number one problem in marriage. If it is not there, a marriage will die a slow death. Lonely is what a husband or wife feels when there is no meaningful interaction between them. Before marriage there was no problem with communication and could talk for hours about everything. In marriage, there are more questions about how to communicate than there are efforts being made in the activity itself.

C. Communication in marriage is like blood to the body. Communication is the lifeblood of marriage. Take it away and you do not have a marriage relationship. Check your communication often to make sure you are not drifting apart. Both marriage partners need to pay attention to the needs they hear from the voice of their mate. If something affects your spouse negatively or positively, you need to know it to eliminate or continue a behavior. Communication allows a spouse to visualize the dreams and interests of their mate (Romans 12:15).

D. Make a list of things important to communication in marriage? _____
_____
_____
_____

What is something **positive** and **encouraging** that you could **say** to your spouse today? What **words** can you use to **lift** his or her spirit? What words of **praise** can you **speak**?

E. Examine the following passages. What does God say is essential in communication?

1. Ephesians 4:15,25 _____
_____

2. Proverbs 15:1 _____
_____

3. James 1:19 _____
_____

4. Proverbs 12:18 _____
_____

5. Ephesians 4:29 _____
_____

6. 1 Peter 3:9 _____
_____

7. James 5:19 _____
_____

8. Hebrews 10:24 _____
_____

F. The Power of Words.

1. Read James 3:5-10. What power does the tongue have? How does the power of the tongue manifest itself in marriage? _____
_____
_____
_____

2. What does Proverbs 18:21 say about the character of the tongue? _____
_____

3. In their book "Building Your Mate's Self-Esteem," Dennis and Barbara Rainey say, "Words are like seeds. Once planted in your mate's life, your words will bring forth flowers or weeds, health or disease, healing or poison..." Your words have the power to contaminate, heal, or spread a disease in your marriage...

4. The value of communication in marriage cannot be overstated. You must be able to speak to one another. You should be comfortable sharing your fears and desires and talk about the relationship itself. Can you do this without criticism, judgment, blaming, accusation, or fear?

5. Many times, when poor communication already exists in marriage, neither spouse can express their dreams or expectations because they "know what the reaction will be." Until you begin to speak without fear of your spouse, you will never be able to share, dream, and help each other.

6. Remember to communicate your need for conversation in a clear, respectful, and forthright way. Do not assume your spouse knows what you are thinking.

7. Stop trying to "read her/his mind." Do not be afraid. Love casts out fear (1 John 4:18). Speak truth to one another in love (Ephesians 4:15). Speak from your heart to your spouse's heart.

8. Words of honesty and openness give hope to every marriage. In Genesis 2:25, "*they were naked, the man and his wife, and were not ashamed.*" Intimacy of the heart, which comes from communication is needed before sexual intimacy. Engaged couples describe their relationship with the following: "we can talk to each other about anything," "she's so easy to talk with," "I can be honest with him and he'll not criticize me," "we're on the same page," "He cares for me," "I trust her/him." If those same words do not describe your marriage, why not? The truest form of intimacy is honest and open communication, before and during marriage.

9. Ten Important Minutes in Communication. Each day, you and your spouse decide how you speak to each other. The most important times of the day in communication are the 5 minutes before you leave each other and the first 5 minutes after you see each other again. The last few words you say before leaving each other are words you think about all day. When you see each other again, the first few words you say to each other set the tone for the remainder of your day together. How do you address your spouse? Are you prepared to greet your spouse? How do you look when you see each other again? Do you touch, kiss, hug, complain, grumble, or keep silent? Is there going to be a conflict? Are you in a rut? Will you build up each other? Do you surprise your mate with something special when you leave or return?

10. A challenge for you. What is something positive and encouraging you could say to your spouse today? What words can you use to lift his or her spirit? What words of praise can you speak? How can you point each other to the truth of God's Word and His promises? _____

_____

_____

G. The Power of Listening.

1. Do you listen to understand your spouse (James 1:19; Proverbs 1:5)?

The **value** of **communi-cation** in **marriage** cannot be overstated. You absolutely **must** be able to **talk** to each **other**.

We take

speech

courses, but not

listening

courses.

Communication

needs both.

2. Couples need to communicate without distraction. How would you apply Matthew 12:30 to listening in marriage? _____ _____

3. Nothing infuriates communication as much as those who are not "with us" in our conversation. Some distractions to listening are children, something on the radio or TV, the phone, computer, texting, etc. All of these hinder valuable "us time." One wife who had trouble with her husband not listening, turned his face toward her with both hands and said, "Listen to me with your face!"

4. A woman falls in love with a man who sets aside time to exchange conversation and affection with her. She stays in love with a man who continues to do it. A husband falls in love with a woman who focuses on his description of his work, accomplishments, and ability. He stays in love with a woman who continues to listen and affirm his endeavors.

5. With every moment of interaction, whether agreement or conflict, ask yourself, "Is this bringing me closer or further away from the person I love?" Listening and making an effort to understand always brings you closer. It helps you and your spouse feel safe, understood, and connected.

6. We take speech courses, but not listening courses. Communication needs both. Try these few listening suggestions: Always put yourself in "listening mode." Focus on him/her. Look at your spouse as they speak. Listen for unspoken fears, concerns, moods, and aspirations. Listen with respect and affirmation. Fight the urge to interrupt. Practice patience. Listen without thinking about how you are going to respond. Listen with regard to your mate's strengths or weaknesses.

H. The Power of Touch.

1. It is hard to sin against someone while you are tenderly touching them. Conversation with touch prevents arguing and it calms the heart. It signals care and brings comfort. Arguing is a cue your communication is not glorifying God.

2. Touching your spouse with both hands helps the communication process.

3. Our culture often associates touch in a sexual context. Some experts believe our extreme preoccupation with sex in this society is actually an expression of our deep, unsatisfied need for the warmth, reassurance, and intimacy of nonsexual touching. A kiss, snuggling, cuddling, holding hands, etc. are some of the first stages of sexual adventure. It should not always lead to sex. Couples need to practice non-sexual forms of touching to communicate their love and emotional connection. This pattern of communication provides a delightful prelude to sexual intimacy.

4. If you desire to communicate effectively in your marriage, consider these non-sexual means: hug, kiss, shoulder rub, back rub, feet rub, stretch across a couch with feet touching or holding the legs of the other.

5. Be "in touch" with your spouse whenever you cannot be with them in person to speak, listen, or touch them. Marriages need "high touch" in a "high tech" society. Writing short love notes or love letters is almost an archaic means of communication for many couples. We are so accustomed to emails, text, and Facebook messages. We rarely post a note or buy a card for our spouse. Staying in constant touch with your spouse electronically has value, but to see your handwriting on paper, bathroom mirror, napkin, in ketchup on a paper plate, water color on art paper, etc. is special. Reading cards or notes from your spouse is a treasure which can never be deleted. They give substance to communication. One lady said regarding her husband's love note: "Seeing his handwriting brings a sense of presence." One husband said about his wife's love notes, "They are part of her that I have to hold. Just seeing her handwriting makes me smile".

I. The Power of Togetherness.

1. Whether by listening, speaking, or touching, communication is illustrated with two circles. Circles which start out separate, not touching. When we share something the two circles touch, intertwine, then overlap. Two separate circles as two people with no common interests, no conversation, separate lives, soon become ONE CIRCLE because they communicate their interests, share their dreams, admire and appreciate one another, grow closer, and pursue one another. With a couple like that communication is easier.

2. If the "airwaves" of communication are open, there are so many benefits in a marriage, not only for staying connected, but also for simply knowing what to expect from each other.

3. If you have *conversation to inform and understand your mate*, you will have achieved one of the secrets to the fine art of communication - connection.

4. Each married partner is capable of doing it. It is not with a conversation starting with "Okay, what do you want to talk about". It is with words to inform, sharing your interests, and being transparent with your spouse. It should be a mate's desire to want to know about their spouse's feelings without responding in criticism, judgment, or blame, but with respect and sensitivity. This way you are able to change your thinking and behavior with the information about your spouse. In this way, you connect in the areas of happy, sad, like, dislike,

worse, better, etc. Learning to change your thinking and behavior with the information about your spouse.

5. By communicating with the goal of connecting, you share the "real you" from the heart. As a result, you establish deep trust, commitment, and friendship. You know you have reached a greater level of communication when your spouse asks, "I think you're angry. Is there something bothering you?," and the answer is not "I'll be alright," but "I think you're right. Maybe what is making me so mad is what my boss said to me in that meeting yesterday." This is the level of communication you want. It takes work to get there.

6. When connecting is your goal in communication, you are not caught up in being "right" because you are focused on the interest of your spouse (Philippians 2:1-4).

7. "Lovemaking" in marriage begins with communication. Make sure your communication skills (i.e. attitude, words, listening, touch, and deeds) are working properly (Philippians 4:8).

8. This evening, set aside some time for true connection. Talk to your husband. Talk to your wife. Listen. Try to understand. Above all, CONNECT. Be connected by the words of Ecclesiastes 4:9-12.

J. Hindrances to Communication in Marriage?

1. What are three great hindrances to good communication in your marriage?
    _____
    _____
    _____

2. The hindrances to communication in most marriages are:

    a. Conversation that punishes your spouse.

    b. Conversation that forces your way.

    c. Conversation that is one-sided.

    d. Conversation that dwells on the past.

    e. Conversation that does not share honestly.

3. Work toward defeating these enemies to communication and protecting your marriage. You can do so by: Admitting your need for communication (whether it is praise, apology, to understand, to help), Believe your spouse is capable of communication (he/she can understand, share, and listen), Confront and Confess. Talk about the issue at hand. Confess "I Need You." Resolve to learn, grow, and love better.

4. Remember. You were not "raised" to communicate. It is not the easiest thing you have ever done. It can be embarrassing and scary. It is highly essential,

and a necessity. Enjoy the journey of communication. Communication pays attention to the needs of your marriage. It is the same way with God. He saw our need for salvation and communicated a truthful, accurate, loving message with power to save us (Romans 1:16). He knew we needed Him and His word communicated to us.

K. Image Builders for Your Marriage.

1. Here is a challenge for you. What is something positive and encouraging you could say to your spouse today? Consider the words you can use to lift his/her spirit? What words of praise can you speak? How can you point each other to the truth of God's Word and His promises?

2. Talk together about how and why it is easy or difficult to share your feelings and become transparent with each other.

3. Schedule a day for the two of you to face each other, hold hands, look at each other in the eye, and say "I Love You" and "I Need You." Give each other time to talk about why you love and need one another.

4. Be sure to take notice when your spouse makes an effort to talk with you. Reinforce their behavior by expressing your appreciation with sincerity and kindness.

5. Commit yourselves to a period of time for reading, talking, listening, and praying together. Do not give up, even if it is difficult at first.

6. Turn a routine activity like shopping, visiting yard sales, traveling, or preparing a meal together into times of conversation.

7. Both of you could spend five to ten minutes per day reading a recommended marriage book together. Afterwards, take five additional minutes to have a positive discussion about what you've read (no criticism allowed). Finish your time together with prayer. Work on this diligently and make it a daily activity.

8. Read the book "The Five Love Languages" by Gary Smalley. From this reading, discover what your spouse's greatest love language is and enjoy "speaking it" to them.

9. Type out a verse of scripture that addresses communication. Post it where you see it every day. Commit it to memory and practice for a week. Repeat the process every week.

10. Some couples have a hard time communicating. The following questions will remove the silence, erase the doubt, and build trust, security, and hope into your marriage. There is a list of questions husbands should ask their wives and and a list wives should ask their husbands every year. Start today.

   a. Ten Questions Every Husband Should Ask His Wife Every Year.

      1. What can I do to cause you to feel more loved and cherished?

2. What can I do to cause you to feel respect for your ideas and your role as a wife?

3. What can I do to assure you I hear you and understand what is on your heart?

4. What can I do to cause you to feel more secure?

5. What can I do to help you feel more confident in our future direction?

6. What attribute would you most like for me to develop?

7. What attribute would you like me to help you develop?

8. What achievement in my life brings you greatest joy?

9. What indicates to you that I really desire to be more Christlike?

10. What mutual goal would you like to see us accomplish?

b. Ten Questions Every Wife Should Ask Her Husband Every Year.

1. Do you feel I properly understand the goals God has placed in your heart? How can I help you achieve them?

2. What are some things I can do regularly to show you I am satisfied with you as my husband and the leader of our home?

3. Is there anything I am doing or failing to do that seems to send a signal that I do not honor you or your leadership in our home?

4. Is there anything I can change to make our home a place where you feel more satisfied and comfortable?

5. Are there any big dreams you have been hesitant to share with me? How can I help you fulfill them?

6. How can we communicate better than we already are?

7. Do you feel there is anything keeping either one or both of us from being what God expects? What is my part in freeing us from those restraints?

8. Are we where you want us to be at this stage in life? How can I help you make it possible within God's guidelines?

9. How do you envision our future together? What can we do together to achieve our goals?

10. What can I do to show you how much I need and trust you?

c. Other questions to consider.

1. If you could store one hour's worth of memory in your mind, which hour of our marriage would you want to remember?

2. If you could have witnessed any biblical event, which one would you choose?

3. Which strengths in your life bring you the greatest satisfaction?

4. What time of day is best for us to talk?

5. If we could just drop what we're doing and go do something fun, what would it be?

6. What is one of the most adventurous things you've ever done?

7. What practical steps can we take to "affair-proof" our marriage?

8. What are five essential values we want our children to embrace?

9. What can we do as a couple to change the world in which we live?

10. What goals would you like us to accomplish in our marriage next year? 5 yrs? 10 yrs?

11. What would you like people to remember about you after your death?

12. What is the first thing that comes to your mind when you think about God?

13. What are five things you are most thankful for in your life right now? What are some of the things you do to show this thankfulness?

14. Whose marriage do you consider to be a model marriage? What is it about their marriage that you admire?

15. What makes a married relationship distinctively Christian? How is a Christian couple different from a non-Christian one?

16. In what ways do you think the marriages of our parents affect our marriage?

17. With many marriages falling apart around us today, what steps can we take to ensure we stay close, emotionally and spiritually?

NOTES:

REFLECTING LOVE IN MARRIAGE

A. What is your definition of love in marriage? _____
_____
_____

B. There are over 17,000 quotes written to define love. Note a few of those quotes.

 1. "Love is the brightest and most beautiful flower in life's garden." - Unknown writer.

 2. "Love is that condition in which the happiness of another person is essential to your own." - Robert A. Heinlein, *Stranger In A Strange Land.*

 3. "'Tis better to have loved and lost, than never to have loved at all." - Alfred Tennyson, "In Memoriam."

 4. "Two people in love, alone, isolated from the world, that's beautiful." - Milan Kundera.

 5. "Love is the irresistible desire to be irresistibly desired." - Mark Twain.

 6. "How do I love thee? Let me count the ways." A phrase characterizing most love letters or poems. These are words by Elizabeth Barrett in the mid-1800s to Robert Browning.

 7. "Love must be learned again and again; there is no end to it. Hate needs no instruction, but waits only to be provoked." - Katherine Anne Porter.

C. The words "I Love You" are not words which automatically hold a marriage together. Those words often describe what we feel about love more than what love

The words **"I Love You"** are **not words** which automatically **hold** a marriage **together**.

is. Married couples realize love must be learned daily. Love is learned from God continually - every day, every season, every year.

D. What Is The Origin Of Real, Marital, Blissful Love?

1. We only have one word in English for love - LOVE. The Greeks had three words.

   a. *Eros* - erotic, sexual, a self-satisfying love. This is most often how our culture defines love.

   b. *Philia* - a love for friendship, acceptance, having same interests. It is where you give a little, get a little - admiration. Like being together because you like or dislike the same things. Problem is, if someone fails to do "their part," the relationship suffers. "I don't love them anymore."

   c. *Agape* - delights in giving, desiring with joy to love another, willing to sacrifice, keeps on loving even if the other is unloveable, unkind, or does not respond. Enduring. Selfless.

2. Marriages need AGAPE love because God is its origin.

   a. What does 1 John 4:19-21 say about the origin and demonstration of love?
   _____
   _____

   b. How does God define love in Matthew 22:34-40? _____
   _____

   c. How does the love God demonstrated help us show love toward our spouse?
   _____
   _____

   d. Many couples struggle and want someone to help them "fix" their spouse. They are wanting a better, fun-filled and intimate marriage, but don't know how to reach it. These couples lack the knowledge that love is a decision. What did God "decide" to do with His love in John 3:16? _____
   _____

   e. Love is not an emotion. Love is not a feeling. Love is not happen-stance. Love is a decision. Love is waking up every day committed to honoring your mate by loving the way God says love should be illustrated. If you want to have a great relationship, it is up to you.

   f. God's love for us generates love in our hearts. God cannot force you to love. His love will cause us to abandon what we thought was love, letting Him fill and control us. Then, real love, agape, will flow through you to those around you, especially your mate.

   g. Although, you may choose to love, you cannot make someone love you. You can show them what love is.

E. Love Is About The Other Person.

1. How wide, deep, broad, and lasting is your love? If you ask a couple before they married how they felt about each other, the answer might be "I love them more than anything in the world. I don't know how I could love them any more than I do now." Fact is, you can and should love them more. The only way to do so is to understand love is not about what the other does to you. Love is about what you do for the other person—what makes him/her happy.

2. Marriage teaches we desired someone *DIFFERENT*. We wanted a *DIFFERENT* person. We accepted the responsibility to love a *DIFFERENT* person. There-fore, one of the challenges to marriage is constantly learning to love *DIFFERENT*.

    a. Loving someone *DIFFERENT* is what Jesus did for us—God dying for man. Read Ephesians 5:25-30 and explain the love of Christ and the love which should be demonstrated in marriage. _____ _____ _____ _____

    b. What does love have to do with sacrificing for your mate? _____ _____ _____

3. Love steps out of your world into his/her world. Jesus did (John 1:14, incarnate love). It is seeing, hearing, and understanding what your spouse experiences (Romans 12:15). Love may not be able to change the situation, but its presence and understanding is priceless.

4. Love is desiring YOUR spouse.

    a. Satan wants our love and friendship. He intention-ally and intently desires it. Through his evil desire, he wants to gain our friendship (James 4:4). He will do anything to get it. God has true love, a desire that is pure, to gain our friendship (1 John 4:7-21). God will not accept love half-way. You cannot have a divided love (Matthew 6:24). Dividing your love between God and Satan meets with disappoint-ment. You need a love for God. A love which thinks about what He wants me to do.

Love is **not** an **emotion**.

Love is not a **feeling**.

Love is not **happenstance**.

Love **is** a **decision**.

    b. Each husband/wife needs the desire to love their spouse - a love for them and them alone. It cannot desire or pursue the love of another (Proverbs 7). Love for your spouse is doing what you can to keep your DESIRE strong for him/her.

    c. 1 Corinthians 7:1-5 shows how this love should be for your spouse alone. DESIRING love is not only about sex; it is about connection, relationship, sharing, exalting the other. What does Genesis 3:16 say about desire? __
_____

    d. To say, "I don't love you anymore" or "I don't desire you anymore" is a failure as a husband/wife. It is not your spouse's fault you don't love them any more.

    e. Your love for your spouse should be as 2 Corinthians 5:14,15. It should *constrain* you to want to do more for your spouse. Therefore, it becomes a joy to be married.

    f. Read 1 John and see how God loves.

    g. How can Philippians 2:1-5 apply to marriage? _____
_____
_____

5. Love is unconditionally committed to the other. Hosea had to do this when God told him to take a harlot as a wife. It was demonstrated by Ruth to Naomi (Ruth 1:16). This means love is concentrated on others in times of joy or sadness, weaknesses and strengths, good and bad, health and sickness, etc.

6. What three ways can you regularly show your spouse you love him/her? ____
_____
_____

7. What is the strongest quality produced by your love for your spouse? _____
_____
_____

8. To have love for the other person requires prayer. For example: "God I need you to teach me to commit, desire, and place myself into my spouse's life. Put the right kind of love in my heart. Make it better than what I have now. Give me strength to let this love grow. Let me be hand in hand in love with Thee and in love with my husband/wife."

9. HUSBANDS ONLY. What does a husband need to do to see his wife as holy, radiant, and without blemish as Christ does his church? _____
_____

10. WIVES ONLY. What does a wife need to do to be more willing and able to respect her husband as the church does Christ? _____
_____
_____

11. HUSBANDS ONLY. What three things can a husband do to convey his love for his wife? _____

_____

12. WIVES ONLY. What three things can a wife do to convey her love for her husband? _____

_____

F. Love Is 1 Corinthians 13:4-8.

   1. The agape love for the other person is illustrated best in this passage.

   2. Be prepared to "describe how love is demonstrated" by studying 1 Corinthians 13:4-8.

     a. "Love suffers long" _____

_____

     b. "Love is kind" _____

_____

     c. "Love envies not" _____

_____

     d. "Love vaunts not self, is not puffed up" _____

_____

_____

     e. "Love does not behave itself unseemly" _____

_____

_____

     f. "Love seeks not her own" _____

_____

     g. "Love is not easily provoked" _____

_____

     h. "Love thinks no evil" _____

_____

     i. "Love rejoices not in iniquity, but rejoices in the truth" _____

_____

_____

     j. "Love bears all things" _____

_____

    k. "Love believes all things" _____
    _____

    l. "Love hopes all things." _____
    _____

    m. "Love endures all things." _____
    _____

    n. "Love never fails." _____
    _____

G. Image Builders for Your Marriage.

1. When a couple is committed to the godly love of 1 Corinthians 13, they will find the greatest thing in the world (v. 13). Will you give God the opportunity to cultivate this love in your marriage? Ask your spouse which of the above characteristics of love would he/she like to see you grow in for the next 6 months.

2. Make time to write your spouse a love letter, not just a quick note, e-mail, text message, or Facebook entry. Hand write a long, more developed expression of love and devotion. When we write a letter, love is placed from heart to hand. Once ink touches paper, it becomes our commitment, a vow to complete.

3. Speak to your spouse's heart, mate's "love language." Give your spouse words of encouragement every day. Praise is such a great gift and easy to give. Look at what makes your spouse unique and say, "thank you."

4. Fight for your spouse's heart and do not destroy it. Conflict will enter your marriage, but it does not have to destroy what you fought to gain. Handling conflict in a respectful way will become the doorway to intimacy. It will deepen your understanding of each other. Instead of becoming your spouse's adversary in conflict and causing your hearts to close to each other, open your hearts to God (James 5:16).

5. Pray to God to embrace, appreciate, and deal with the differences in a loving way. Ask God to open your heart to show you how those differences can build your marriage, rather than criticize them because they are different.

6. Care for your spouse's heart. Keep the promise you made in your wedding vows to care for each other. Communicate and agree on when it is a good time to talk. Respect how valuable and vulnerable your spouse's heart is by treating it gently. Express empathy ("I feel what you are feeling and I want to share in your joy or pain.") and affirm what your spouse is experiencing ("What you are feeling matters to me and you matter to me.")

7. Ask your spouse how you can best demonstrate love to him/her? Seek ways to practice it.

8. Purchase the "*Love Dare*" book from the movie *FIREPROOF*. Meet the challenge of reading and transforming your marriage by practicing unconditional love for the next 40 days. Once you are done, repeat the process. Enjoy the results.

9. Train yourself in how to have love and keep love by applying the list below.

Having Love and Keeping Love In Marriage

- Learn the art of touching—tenderly.

- Continue to court your spouse always.

- Build—or rebuild—trust in your relationship.

- Praise is a great gift and easy to give. So, look at the things that make your spouse great and unique. Develop the habit of praising him/her for those special things.

- Desire his/her love only.

- Love is about the other person.

- Compliment your mate in front of friends or family.

- Put down everything to greet your spouse at the end of the day.

- Hide love notes around the house where your spouse will find them.

- Get to know your in-laws.

- Let the love of Christ constrain you (2 Cor 5:14).

- Know the origin of love - God (1 Jn 4:19).

- Verbally reassure your spouse of your commitment to him/her.

- Acknowledge your sin and weaknesses.

- Be spiritually minded and obedient.

- Pray with and for your spouse every day.

- Enjoy a "date" with your spouse.

- Spend 10 minutes each day listening to your spouse share his/her day.

- Discover and fulfill three ways your spouse likes you to show affection.

- Say "thank you" often about something your spouse has done for you.

- Give your spouse 15 minutes per day to ask you any question and answer each question honestly.

- Tell your spouse each week what you specifically appreciate about him/her.

- Spend 5 uninterrupted minutes each week telling your spouse what you specifically appreciate about him/her.

- Ask your spouse what domestic chore he or she would like you to do for him/her and do it.

- Call your spouse a minimum of four times during the week to see how he/she is, and if there is something you can do for him/her.

- Tell your spouse these three great words, "I Need You" at least 3 times a week.

- Write a short love note. Place it where your spouse will most likely see it.

THE IMAGE OF ROMANCE AND SEX IN A COUPLE OF SAINTS

A. Where did you learn your first lessons about romance and/or sex? _____

B. Do you hold the same view toward romance and sex today? Why or why not? _____
_____
_____

C. When Christians marry and understand the role, the blessing, and the holiness of sex in marriage, it becomes a positive, sacred power for good. Romance and sex are embraced with a new enthusiasm and purpose. When couples experience sexual intimacy on the level of what a Christian should, they fully live out God's design for intimacy. They create more ideas and avenues of romance where the idea of infidelity is completely gone. Godly, positive, and holy sexual experiences are like pulling the weeds of temptation out of the ground.

D. God's design of sex in marriage destroys the myth about sex being a "one-sided" issue—more of a "man thing" than a "woman thing." God designed it for both the man and the woman. How both the man and the woman are connected to romance and sex in marriage varies.

E. Every husband and wife should have a godly view of sex as an honored blessing to keep the marital connection strong. Studies have shown a one-to-one connection between the frequency of sexual intercourse within a marriage and the overall satisfaction of that marriage. Is that a surprise? Not when you look at Genesis 2:25 and Hebrews 13:4. The results of the study reflect what is literally happening to a couple's brains when they engage in the physical expression of their love and why premarital sexual experience preserves an ungodly

> Every **husband** and **wife** should have a **godly view** of **sex** as an **honored blessing** to keep the marital **connection strong**.

relationship (1 Corinthians 6:16-18). God knew what He was talking about when he prescribed sexual experience only for marriage.

F. Each couple should understand satisfying sex is not just about you and your spouse. It is not just about affair-proofing your marriage. It is about reflecting and pleasing the ultimate engineer, the God who thought it all up in the first place. For a married Christian, there is no greater joy.

G. Romance: Touching the Heart Before Touching the Body.

1. Read Genesis 2:25. Why would Adam and Eve not be ashamed lying naked beside one another? Adam and Eve touched each other's heart before they touched each other's body.

2. When asked to describe the purpose of romance, a woman may use words such as friendship, tenderness, relationship, and endearment. She wants her heart touched before having her body caressed. Given the same question, a man usually answers with one of the shortest words in the English language—sex. For him, physical oneness and affirmation of his manhood equal romance. Can two people with such different perspectives have their expectations met? Absolutely!

3. Our culture tends to view romance and sex in a lustful way, making it look satisfying only outside marriage. It makes romance and sex in marriage bland, routine, ritual, or duty. In the Middle Ages, the context for romantic love was never in marriage. In the love ballads, the poetry of the high Middle Ages, it was in illicit affairs where men had affairs with women, married or not. A lot of the secular love poetry of the Medieval Period was adulterous. Marriage was seen as a place to procreate children and illustrate the union of Christ and His Church. It was not viewed as a romantic, loving companionship. This was not God's way.

4. One couple, who had been married for 37 years, evaluated what they had been through over the past few years. They decided, "We need to have some fun—just some pure, laugh-all-the-time type of fun. We are on a mission right now over the next 6 to 12 months to find ways we can have fun...we are yearning for the companionship based on problem solving, it is not about duty. It is really a matter of sharing life with someone you really do enjoy."

5. Baking a cake is a matter of putting together all the right ingredients, using "trial and error", trying again, etc. Love "baking" your marriage, and never stop working to perfect the recipe for romance. True lovemaking is the coming together of emotional, spiritual, and physical oneness.

6. Give your spouse romantic attention. Do not allow for complacency. Being tired cannot always be an excuse. Children are not to blame. Too many try to rush and squeeze romance and sex into a small segment of their busy lives.

7. Without romance in your marriage, sex becomes just an *act*. Romance supports what the sexual union brings to a married couple. This means the *relationship*

has to have top priority in order for sexual intimacy to mean something more than an act.

8. What hinders romance in marriage? _____
_____
_____

H. How Sex Points Us To God.

1. Is God's design for sex in marriage (a) for sexual pleasure, (b) for procreation, (c) to reflect the image of God, (d) all the above ? Scripturally explain your answer. _____
_____

2. Believe it or not, making love with your spouse is a spiritual as well as a physical exercise.

3. What does Hebrews 13:4 say about the marriage bed? _____

4. The holiness of sex in marriage should exalt your marriage into a state of honor, respect, and admiration. It needs to have this valuable place in your heart. This is because your marriage is a reflection of God's image.

5. The spirituality of sex in marriage is God-given and something many do not understand. Most see sex as a physical event enjoyed by husband and wife. Although sex is a physical act of pleasure, it is a holy, spiritual connection with God. God does not turn His eyes when a husband and wife are in the bed. Neither should you turn yours away from God when you share your body with your mate. This is God's idea for sexual feelings and fulfillment being reserved for marriage. God calls this part of His creation "very good" (Genesis 1:31). You can become content and at peace with what God has given you in marriage.

6. Notice the following ways to glorify God through pursuing sexual intimacy with your spouse.

   a. *Replace guilt with gratitude.* Past sexual experiences bring guilt, hurt, and regret hindering us spiritually and blocking sexual intimacy with our spouse. When the world abuses sex, it leaves Christians with the idea that sex is inherently evil. Combine this with any previous negative experiences, sex feels evil. Those attitudes have to be

Each couple should understand **satisfying sex** is not just about you and your spouse... It is about **reflecting** and **pleasing** the ultimate engineer, the **God** who thought it all up in the first place.

turned into gratitude to God for this amazing experience and holy act. Satisfying sex is found only within God's parameters. When you give a gift to someone, how do you feel as you see that person enjoy and appreciate the gift? In this same way, God created sex for pleasure and lifelong enjoyment in marriage. Sex is to be awed, not considered awful. How do you believe gratitude for sex within marriage helps people overcome guilt caused by sexual experiences (sexual abuse, affair, pornography, etc.) apart from marriage? _____

_____

b. *Protect what God created* for sexual joy in marriage. Notice six sexual practices God forbids.

   1. Sex outside of marriage - adultery, fornication.

   2. Sex with a member of the same sex: homosexuality.

   3. Sex with a member of your family: incest.

   4. Sex with animals: bestiality.

   5. Sex fantasies or desires for someone other than your spouse, which is found in pornography of any kind, as well as mentally playing out lustful fancies for real or imaginary men/women.

   6. Sex that finds pleasure in pain or violence - rape, sadomasochism, brutality.

      Read 1 Corinthians 10:23. How does the principle found in this verse apply to sexuality in marriage? _____

      _____

      _____

      Think of all the benefits we receive from fire such as warmth, light, and beauty. Imagine the devastating effects of a fire raging out of control. Sexuality is very similar to a fire. When we follow the guidelines God has established for sex, we experience deep levels of intimacy, communication, and fulfillment. If sex moves out of God's parameters, it yields destruction, pain, regret, and possibly death.

c. *Pray together* with your spouse in thanks for the pleasure surrounding marital consummation.

d. *Sex is an expression of ONENESS.* Read 1 Corinthians 6:15-18. If being joined to a harlot is ONENESS, what is being joined to your Spouse? ____

   _____

   1. Romance and sex have new meaning when you join *sanctified* bodies in the presence of God thru marriage. Joining yourself to a prostitute, to someone already married, to someone not married, or to someone

of the same sex is not allowed because your body is a holy temple. Therefore, when two saints of God are joined in sexual intimacy, it is a holy union.

2. ONENESS is the emotional, spiritual, and sexual intimacy of marriage. Sex is the seal of commitment to your marriage covenant before God (consummate, complete, perfect). You are mine. I am yours.

3. Genesis 2 describes the two becoming one, naked, and not ashamed. A ONENESS in marriage is created. Your spouse is not simply an "object of pleasure" for your sexual satisfaction. It is a holy and sacred union designed by God (Hebrews 13:4), where its fulfillment is only upon "holy ground" – your bed.

e. *View your spouse as "fearfully and wonderfully made"* (Psalm 139:14). Our world is addicted to the body. The more one exposes his/her body only magnifies immorality, abuse, and adultery. It allows for sexual drives to run rampant giving people permission to stare, talk about, and lust at sexually as much as possible. How would 2 Corinthians 10:5 help a husband and wife's attitude toward their mate's body? _____

_____

_____

f. One man said, *"If a woman is beautiful under the age of 40, she had something to do with it. If she's beautiful after the age of 40, her husband had something to do with it."* Attitude toward your mate's body is paramount. Your spouse needs to know how much he/she is loved, cared for, and accepted sexually just the way God created them. Being "fit" for each other is the beauty of sex. It is not that you would be happier simply because he/she was thinner, shaped different, etc. Having a godly attitude toward your spouse made in the image of God, keeps your thoughts pure and keeps your mate from feeling they have to compete with the world. If you are having trouble in being happy with your spouse's body, examine your head and heart.

g. *Realize the power and pleasure of sex.* God gave sex a unique power every couple should appreciate, value, and harness. It is created by God to preserve marriage and keep alive the bonds of affection between husband and wife.

Read 1 Corinthians 7:1-5. How does this passage help us understand the power and pleasure of sex in marriage? _____

_____

_____

h. Note the following points from 1 Corinthians 7:1-5.

1. Sexual fulfillment is part of the marriage covenant – an agreement of husband and wife.

2. Sexual needs are given equal value and consideration. No one is a sex slave or toy.

3. Depriving this need demands three things (a) agreement to abstain, (b) abstinence is temporary, and (c) abstinence period should be a prayerful time (dedicated to purity, holiness, and commitment to your spouse).

4. Married couples should return to sexual activity before temptation overpowers either spouse. EX: traveling, couples with younger children, a spouse may be ill or worn-out. It would be unkind or impossible to place sexual expectations on a husband or wife under these circumstances.

5. Each spouse holds sexual power. This power is not to be abused or used as a means of manipulating the conscience of your mate. Remember, there are spiritual implications to how each couple considers the power of sex in marriage.

6. Respect sexual power. Love it. Connect with it. Be satisfied with it. Use its power exclusively for your marriage in order to reflect the image of God.

I. Sexually Serve your Spouse.

1. How does selfishness affect a married couple with regard to their sex life? __
   _____
   _____

2. What impact does an attitude of service have upon sex in marriage? _____
   _____
   _____

3. *Give what you have exclusively.* Continuing to give your body to your spouse even when you believe it constitutes "damaged goods" can be rewarding spiritually. "*Marriage teaches us to give what we have. God has given us one body. He has commanded our spouse to delight in that one body—and that body alone,*" Gary Thomas, "Sacred Marriage" writes. What are the implications of that statement for taking care of your body and for appreciating your spouse's body? _____
   _____
   _____

4. Jesus had "*all things*" in His hand (John 13:3). Instead of abusing it or withdrawing it, He got up, took a towel and washed His disciples feet. WHY? Because He came to serve, not to be served (Mark 10:45).

5. Serving your spouse sexually comes from an attitude of humility and selflessness. It is about serving each other. It is God providing you a way to serve your mate in marriage. Be pleased with how you serve your spouse and you

will be pleased in return (Matthew 7:12). If you choose not to romance your spouse, you will not be romanced.

6. To serve your mate, reserve your thoughts, attitudes, and desires for him/her. The only sex life your spouse can and should enjoy is the one you give him/her. When the passions for sex in marriage come alive, do not fear it, embrace it.

7. To fully embrace marital sexuality in all the ways God designed it, a couple must bring their Christianity into bed and break down the wall between their physical and spiritual intimacy. Developing a fulfilling sex life means you concern yourself more with bringing generosity and service to bed than with bringing a washboard abdomen or smooth, silky hair. You see your husband/ wife as a holy temple of God, not just a beautiful, hot, sexy body. Satisfying sex is not just about you and your spouse or affair-proofing your marriage, but about serving your spouse and serving the God who designed it. God created a freedom to explore and enjoy sexual intimacy. The journey is along a path of faith, grace, and service to your spouse. For a believer, there is no guilt with this, but great joy. It provides the opportunity to have the spiritual connection God wants you to have with your spouse.

J. Image Builders for Your Marriage.

1. Place yourself in a romantic setting at least twice a week, have a couple of date nights a month, and a couple of get-away nights a year.

2. Discuss with your spouse specific behaviors he/she would like to see you change to be more romantic and sexual in your marriage? Specifically ask your spouse, "Is there anything I am currently doing that is offensive to you or you would rather not do? Is there something you would like to do that we are not currently doing?"

3. Spend time discussing with your spouse how you can fulfill each other sexually.

4. List ten ways your spouse can be romantic to you. Give your list to your spouse, then be creative in fulfilling this list.

5. Pray with your spouse with gratitude to God for His gift of sex. Ask Him to guide you to be unselfish in satisfying your mate.

6. HUSBANDS: Read the book "For Men ONLY" (Jeff and Shaunti Feldhahn). WIVES: Read the book "For Women ONLY" (Shaunti Feldhahn). These books help husbands and wives understand the romantic and sexual needs of each other.

7. If you would like "12 Dates to Romance Your Mate", make your request by email (kampkennessee@juno.com) and it will be sent to you.

8. As an assignment, read through the Song of Solomon and make notes together about each chapter. List lessons you learned about romance and sex in marriage.

NOTES:

10 IDEAS FOR INCREASING ROMANCE

These 10 ideas will help bring back the desire you enjoyed as a couple early in your relationship. These suggestions make your character more attractive to your spouse.

1. *Communicate.* Talk to each other. Share your thoughts and expose your feelings instead of keeping them to yourself. Do this without distractions (children, TV, radio, phone, etc. – Ephesians 4:15,25,29).

2. *Extend forgiveness regularly.* Nothing ruins a desire to be with your spouse faster than resentment and bitterness. In return, it also ruins your spouse's desire to be with you. Conflicts happen in marriage, so choose to resolve these conflicts in the right way and improve your marriage (Ephesians 4:31-32).

3. *Live selflessly.* As followers of Christ, we are called to be servants (Galatians 5:13). This applies to the church body, our neighbors, and marriage. If you put your husband's or wife's needs above your own, you will find that you argue less, and pity yourself less; causing your children to feel secure and happy (Philippians 2:1-5).

4. *Use words of affirmation regularly.* The tongue is a powerful tool. James 3:6 tells us that the tongue has the ability to defile the whole body and set on fire the course of a man's life. Look for and express your mate's positivie attributes. Take the opportunity to express your heartfelt appreciation. Give some praise because it goes a long way.

5. *Never stop saying, "I love you."* No comment necessary. It speaks for itself.

6. *Laugh together.* Marriage is about friendship, relationship, and companionship. Do fun things together and funny things together. Proverbs 17:22 says, "A joyful heart is good medicine, but a broken spirit dries up the bones." Make room for a little laughter in your marriage.

7. *Tame your thoughts.* Control your thought processes. Sex begins in the mind. Let your desires be only for your spouse (1 Corinthians 7:1-5). Think about your mate ONLY.

8. *Pray together.* Spiritual intimacy is more important than physical intimacy. Many couples have regular sexual activity, but are not intimate—they miss out on the soul of the person. Christ is the bond that makes a marriage strong and sturdy. When the spiritual part of a relationship is sturdy and strong, it lays the foundation for healthy sexual intimacy.

9. *Check your expectations.* Make sure your expectations from your mate are in accordance with the abilities God has given them. There is nothing wrong with goals and objectives. Help one another reach the goals together.

10. *Also believe and say to each other, "We're going to make it!"* Marriage is a covenant made to last until death. This may be hard to believe in a culture where divorce is commonplace, but the Word of God is serious about the promise of vows between man and wife (Matthew 19:3-9). Never threaten to leave. Love never fails.

REFLECTING FORGIVENESS IN MARRIAGE

A. Answer the following with either TRUE or FALSE.

1. Every couple will have a fight in marriage _____.

2. Conflicts are natural in marriage _____.

3. Every couple is destined to argue _____.

B. Answer the following with either TRUE or FALSE.

1. With the design and makeup of the church, every church will have conflict _____.

2. The church is destined to have a fight _____.

3. The conclusion of Ephesians 4:1-3 is division of the church _____.

C. Read James 4:1,2. Why does conflict exist in marriage? _____ _____

D. List five of the most common areas of conflict in marriage. _____ _____ _____ _____ _____

If you and your spouse are **in** constant **conflict**, get off the bulldozer and **stop running over** your **spouse**.

E. Conflict in marriage comes from an attempt to gain control, manipulate, or win a victory. Its origin comes from selfish feelings about something you feel strongly. Conflicts are brought on by an expectation not met, a need unfulfilled, hurt feelings, or past experiences (he/she did this before).

F. If, through your "wars," you have punished your spouse to get what you want and gained a victory, at what price did you win? You may have "won," but it is really an empty victory because the one you have defeated is your spouse.

G. Steady doses of conflicts in marriage move couples into:

1. Denial - pretend a problem does not exist (1 Samuel 2:22-25).

2. Flee - run away, pull away, quit, withdraw, go to another room, go to the shop, go shopping, etc.

3. Suicide - When a spouse loses all hope of resolving a conflict, their escape may be an attempt to take their own life (1 Samuel 31:4). Suicide is never a right way to deal with conflict.

4. Some couples move toward attacking their spouse because they would rather control their mate than preserve their relationship by:

a. Assault - using some form of force or intimidation by physical violence or verbal attacks (i.e. gossip, slander, blame; EX: Council against Stephen – Acts 6:8-15);

b. Lawsuit - restraining orders, legal separations, divorce (read Matthew 5:25,26; 1 Corinthians 6:1-8).

c. Murder - In an extreme effort to win, murder may be attempted (EX: Stoning of Stephen – Acts 7:54-58). A spouse may even "kill" their spouse in their heart (see Matthew 5:21,22; 1 John 3:15).

H. The result of most conflicts is a lack of respect, no affection, no sex, spite, anger, bitterness, jealousy, blame, criticism, etc. If you are in constant conflict, get off the bulldozer and stop running over your spouse.

I. The one character trait revealed in conflict is ANGER. Ephesians 4:26 says, "*Be ye angry, and sin not: let not the sun go down upon your wrath.*" Anger is proper and needed, but in conflict its use is abused. There is something about ANGER every couple needs to understand. Anger can be hidden in resentment, aggression, frustration, hate, fury, indignation, outrage, wrath, antagonism, crossness, hostility, bitterness, destructiveness, spite, rancor, ferocity, scorn, disdain, enmity, and defiance.

J. The above attitudes often define the anger in conflict, feeling justified because of the hurt.

K. Once the angry attitudes are in place, the way in which it is communicated is hate, wound, damage, annihilate, despise, scorn, disdain, loathe, vilify, curse, despoil, ruin, demolish, abhor, abominate, desolate, ridicule, tease, kid, get even, laugh at, humiliate, goad, shame, criticize, cut, take out spite on, rail at, scold, bawl out, humble, irritate, beat up, take for a ride, ostracize, fight, beat, vanquish, compete with, brutalize, crush, offend, and bully.

L. Regardless of the term you use, it is still anger. Anger does NOT represent the attitude couples should have toward one another. This is NOT the attitude to resolve a conflict.

M. Notice the escalation of a conflict below:

   1. Differences of Opinion - "Spat" - Confrontation.

   2. Heated Debate or Argument - "Quarrel" - Division.

   3. Intense Anger Expressed - "Fight" - Rejection.

   4. Hostility Confirmed - "War" - Separation.

N. Times of conflict do not have to be destructive. Rightly used, they become the growing edges of your relationship. It points you to the areas where work is needed to make your marriage richer and deeper. Conflict comes because we are unique and different individuals with different tastes, habits, likes and dislikes, and values and standards. However, when you point your "weapons" at the problem rather than each other, you achieve an understanding, appreciation, and respect of your spouse and a resolution. If the issues are ignored or suppressed, the stage is set for a painful explosion. Often times unresolved conflicts have attitudes of pride, selfishness, and suspicion. Then in the next conflict, the past resurfaces (i.e. "I remember the last time you...," "You did this before...").

O. How was conflict handled in your parents' marriage? _____
   _____
   _____

P. Some of the stages of conflict you experience may be similar to what you witnessed as a child. Therefore, this may be how you handle it in your marriage. One of the following characterizes you and your marriage when conflict arises.

   1. Withdrawal: may be physically or psychological.

   2. Winning: the goal no matter what the cost.

   3. Yielding: giving in, being the loser or martyr.

   4. Compromise: give a little, get a little, bargaining.

   5. Resolve: spend time through communication resolving a conflict to a mutually agreeable solution.

   Compromise and resolution accomplish the most for a marriage. How you handle conflict depends on the value placed on your relationship. Review the five styles of conflict above and ask which style is reflected in your marriage?

The following diagram shows how unresovled conflict creates an unending cycle...

Differences ⟶ Disagreement ⟶ Conflict ⟶ Resolution

Avoidance of real issues

Q. Let's learn to recognize and improve our individual patterns of conflict.

R. Ephesians 4 and Conquering Conflict.

1. If you could change the manner in which you and your spouse handle conflict, what would you change? _____
_____
_____

2. What "rules" have you and your spouse established when conflict arises in your marriage (EX: do not yell)? _____
_____
_____

3. When is the "wrong time" to resolve a conflict? When is the "right time" to resolve a conflict? _____
_____
_____

4. Consider the following guidelines for resolving conflict in marriage.

   a. Do not avoid conflict with "the silent treatment!"

   b. Do not save up emotional trading stamps and exchange them with a "piece of your mind!"

   c. Do not strike while the iron is "hot"—at the wrong time or place!

   d. Do not attack your mate. Attack the problem!

   e. Do not throw your feelings like stones or "hit below the belt."

   f. Do not get off the topic or drag other issues or people into the problem.

   g. Do not criticize without offering solutions.

   h. Do not tell your spouse what he/she feels or thinks or "should" feel or think.

   i. Never say "You never...You always...You can't..." or use sarcasm, exaggerations, hysterical statements, or name calling!

   j. Never let pride take over. You just may be wrong!

5. Read Ephesians 4. Consider how the verses listed below could help you resolve conflict in marriage.

    a. Verses 1 – 3 _____

    b. Verses 4 – 6 _____

    c. Verses 11, 12 _____

    d. Verses 13, 14 _____

    e. Verses 15, 25 _____

    f. Verse 16 _____

    g. Verses 17 – 19 _____

    h. Verses 20 – 24 _____

    i. Verses 26, 27 _____

    j. Verse 29 _____

    k. Verses 30 – 32 _____

6. How did Jesus handle conflict in the following passages?

    a. Matthew 15:1-9 _____

    b. Mark 11:11-19 _____

    c. John 8:1-11 _____

7. How would James 1:19–20 impact a couple's ability to resolve conflict? ____
    _____
    _____

8. Read the following passages and note how these passages help a couple in conflict (Proverbs 3:30; 15:18; 17:14,19; 18:6; 20:3; 2 Timothy 2:14, 16, 24; Philippians 2:3). _____
    _____
    _____
    _____

9. Read 1 Peter 3:8-12. In what way would this passage help bring a couple who is in conflict toward closeness. _____
    _____
    _____
    _____

10. Some important facts about handling conflict are:

   a. Begin handling a conflict with a prayer, asking God's help to direct your thoughts, words, attitudes, reception, and open your heart to resolution.

   b. Introduce the handling of your conflict with three genuine words - "I love you."

   c. Choose the right time and place to handle the conflict.

   d. Establish "rules of the house" when an argument begins.

   e. Learn to listen with complete attention (i.e. be present in the moment). Exercise patience.

   f. State clearly what you see is happening in the conflict. State the points upon which you agree. Feelings are a part of conflict, but do not let them overrule the facts.

   g. Learn to "own" the problem and the part you have in the conflict.

   h. Use "I" statements rather than "You" statements.

   i. Never withhold physical intimacy from your spouse as a means of manipulation (1 Corinthians 7:5).

   j. Conclude your discussion with a "sign" - a word, a touch, affirmation, celebration, prayer.

   k. If after discussing the matter, differences remain, affirm you agree to disagree, or offer to give your spouse what they need from you with generosity, not grudgingly.

S. Forgiveness: The Picture of Reconciliation.

   1. STORY: Two men were hiking on a mountain trip. There was a fast-moving creek to cross. One of the men gave his friend this advice, "When you jump across, make sure you fall forward. Keep your momentum going forward so you won't get swept away in the stream."

   2. When conflicts arise in a marriage, the most common response is to pull back or distance yourself. What you can do is control the direction in which you fall—toward your spouse. This attitude needs to prevail if any conflict in marriage is to be resolved. It is a reflection of the image of God. God continually falls forward toward us and a couple needs to understand the value of this. In Romans 5:6-8, how did God move toward us as sinners? _____
   _____

   3. How does the way God deals with the sin of man help YOU with the mistakes and weaknesses of YOUR spouse? Read Colossians 3:13. _____
   _____

Reconciliation should be your goal in resolving conflict with your spouse just as it was with God when He was "reconciling the world unto himself" (2 Corinthians 5:19).

4. A couple can make the choice early and say "I'm going to forgive" or feel hurt, refuse to address the pain, deny the strife, play the victim, issue blame, or resort to bitterness.

5. What did the father do for his son in Luke 15:11-32? Forget about him or fall forward? _____
    _____

6. Reconciling and Fellowship with your mate should be your desire once a conflict has divided and hurt your marriage. It is a matter of hating the sin, but loving the "sinner." Every marriage has to grab and hold on to this statement. It is not a matter of who "goes first." It is what is first – your marriage or your pride. This is why marriage cannot be approached with "self-righteousness," but extending grace and mercy. Unless you love mercy (Micah 6:8), you will have a hard time extending it to your spouse.

7. Read Matthew 18:21-35. What lessons can a marriage learn about forgiveness from this passage? _____
    _____
    _____

8. Read Matthew 6:14,15. What is the implication of showing mercy or being unmerciful to my spouse? _____
    _____

9. Read Luke 17:1-5. How often should my mate sin, repent and be forgiven? __
    _____
    _____

10. Forgiveness given or neglected in marriage determines whether you have the attitude to show the same to others outside your marriage.

11. Today, can you say YOUR response to the mistakes of your spouse due to a conflict has remained the same, gotten worse, or gotten better in the last year of your marriage? _____

T. The Spiritual Guide and Impact of Forgiveness.

1. Conflict provides four significant opportunities

    a. *Glorify God by obeying and imitating Him* (1 Corinthians 10:31). Daily efforts made to prevent or resolve conflict comes from an attitude which asks "How can I please and honor the Lord in this situation?" Read Ephesians 5:1,2. What is the attitude every couple should have when resolving conflict in marriage? _____

    b. *Get the Beam Out of Your Own Eye* (Matthew 7:1-5). Why is this important to a couple attempting to resolve a conflict in their marriage? _____

_____

_____

The "beams" often witnessed in marriage conflicts involve sinful words and actions. Sometimes we cannot see what we are doing or hear what we are saying. See what contribution you made to the conflict. One way to do this is to use the Seven A's of Confession.

a)   Address your spouse, not everyone else. He/she is the one affected.

b)   Avoid "if, but, and maybe" words. Do not try to excuse your wrongs.

c)   Admit specifically - whatever attitudes and actions of which you are guilty.

d)   Acknowledge the hurt. Express "sorrow" for hurting your husband/wife.

e)   Accept the consequences. Say, "I'm sorry. I was wrong."

f)   Alter your behavior. Make the change in your attitudes and actions.

g)   Ask for forgiveness (1 John 1:8,9). Grow your marriage to reflect the image of God by being like Christ, by confessing sin, and by turning from attitudes promoting conflict.

c.   *Serve your spouse by restoring them to fellowship* (Matthew 5:23,24; James 5:19,20). Help bear their burdens or confront them in love. Read Matthew 18:15. What example of restoration is given in vv. 12-14? _____
Our effort in resolving a conflict is to "win" our spouse, not win a war. To do so, an attitude of serving needs to accompany the effort to resolve the conflict by bringing your spouse back to you as a shepherd does his wandering sheep (Galatians 6:1). Go toward your spouse. Pursue the relationship. Pride allows a spouse to suffer in weakness, pain, sin, or wrong. A merciful heart wants renewal. Restoration is not accomplished with "I forgive her. I just won't ask her to do anything for me again. I'll do it myself!" Instead, forgive totally and openly – "I forgive you and I want back what we had before. I need you."

d.   *Make solid your promise to forgive.* You imitate God's forgiveness when you forgive as He does (Hebrews 8:12; 1 John 1:9). To make that a reality, there are four promises that must be made to your spouse to keep from punishing him/her in the future.

a)   "I will not dwell on this incident."

b)   "I will not bring up this incident again and use it against you."

c)   "I will not talk to others about this incident."

d)   "I will not let this incident stand between us or hinder our personal relationship."

These promises tear down the walls which stand between you and your spouse. The way is cleared for your relationship to develop unhindered by memories of past wrongs. Learn from the past and move toward each other. It is His will for us to move toward our spouse.

2. Forgiveness is a spiritual process that cannot be accomplished on your own. As you seek to forgive your spouse, continually ask God for grace to enable you to imitate His wonderful forgiveness toward you.

3. Apology + Forgiveness = Reconciliation. This is a picture of choice. You choose to paint this image of God in your marriage. When godly sorrow lives within the context of your marriage (2 Corinthians 7:9,10), you will not be defensive. You will be the first to say, "Let's end this!"

4. "A happy marriage is the union of two good forgivers."

5. "To carry a grudge is like being stung to death by one bee."

6. "Forgiveness is like paying off a debt, tearing up the note, burning it, never to see it again."

7. You cannot go back and undo a quarrel, battle, or conflict. You cannot go back and start a new beginning. You can start today and make a new ending.

8. You owe it to yourself and your marriage to forgive. If you fail to do so, you burn the bridge to your forgiveness from God.

9. Read Mark 2:9. "Which is easier...?" Which is easier, apologize to your wife because you did not fill up the car with gas or blame her because you are in a hurry and don't have time to fill it up? Which is easier, apologize to your husband for saying, "You're irrational," or say, "I did exaggerate too much!"

10. Are there matters of principle which should not be compromised and matters of preference which should be subject to compromise within a marriage? If so, what are they? _____
_____
_____

11. Of the following, which do YOU believe is the most difficult part of forgiveness:

    a. Forgiving yourself? Why? _____
    _____

    b. Forgiving your spouse? Why? _____
    _____

12. What do you believe are the long-term benefits of learning to fall toward your spouse rather than away from him/her? _____
_____
_____
_____

U. Image Builders for Your Marriage.

1. Have a conflict resolution date to work through some issues which trouble your marriage.

2. If you have not written out a set of "Rules for Conflict" for your marriage, do so.

3. Admit your need to resolve a conflict. Believe your spouse is capable of resolving it with you. Confront the sin and Confess your part in the conflict.

4. Pay attention to your marriage.

5. Study together God's means of forgiving, reconciliation, and desire to have fellowship with each other. Write down how those principles can positively impact your marriage when conflict occurs.

6. Have a "WE" attitude toward your marriage, not a "You" attitude toward your spouse.

7. Remember in all your conflicts, your mate is not your enemy. Satan is. What God hath joined together, let not man put asunder (Matthew 19:6).

8. They need your help...
   After only two years of marriage, Nancy and John are living very separate lives. The problem? Neither of them likes conflict, so they avoid each other. Nancy pours herself into hobbies and caring for their nine-month-old son. John is staying later at work, and often goes straight from there to the health club. On those nights, he doesn't even see Nancy or his son before they go to bed. Using the excuse he doesn't want to disturb his wife, he sleeps on the couch. John and Nancy can't remember when they last had a night out together. Their sexual intimacy has dwindled to once or twice a month, with little tenderness or joy. Both are concerned about their marriage, but feel immobilized by the fear of getting angry, getting hurt, or hurting each other. How would you help John and Nancy resolve this conflict?

NOTES:

MARRIAGE TEACHES US TO REFLECT PERSEVERANCE

A. Read Matthew 19:1-6. From this text, what is the primary lesson(s) a couple should understand about the endurance of their marriage? _____
_____

B. Read Philippians 3:12-16. From this text, how does a couple have a lasting marriage? _____
_____
_____

C. Jesus exhorted the Pharisees to protect their marriage from divorce by looking at God's design. They tried to find an exception and not follow the rule. They thought about how to get out of the marriage rather than stay in it.

D. Would you marry your spouse again? It was a question asked of 3,000 women by Woman's Day magazine and AOL.com. 44% said they would marry their husbands again, 36 % said "No," 20% were unsure. Over half would not or were unsure. ABOUT.com has an ongoing survey with the question, "Would you marry your spouse again?" 25% - YES; 56% - NO; 16% - Don't Know - (12319 votes - 3-6-15).

E. Living in a world where people become discontent easily from TV programs, preachers, electronics, and games, is it any wonder spouses are not content with their mate, nor have the desire to protect them or their marriage? Some spouses treat each other as if they will always be there. When you hear advertisements implying we deserve a "new," "improved," and "better" anything, people think the same way about their marriage. As a result, there is a failure to protect what God makes sacred, holy, and sanctified.

If your **marriage** with the **ONE** you chose is **not growing** and **developing** as it should, the reason may be **because** you have **gone against** some **biblical** instructions.

F. Nothing damages the heart of marriage more than the words, "I'm not in love with you any more," "Our marriage is over," "I want out," "I can't take it any more," "I don't have any feelings for you anymore," "You're not the woman/man I married." How could these words come from someone who just a few weeks, months, or years ago said, "I will," "I do," "until death shall separate us?"

G. Every couple needs to make their marriage last a lifetime, and protect it. So, there would be no hesitation to say, "I would marry my spouse again." Obtaining this prize, like obtaining heaven, requires more than just you. In Ecclesiastes 4:9-12, what helps make an enduring marriage? _____
_____

H. Marriage is supposed to last forever. What keeps marriages from lasting until "death do us part?" _____
_____
_____

I. The goal of marriage is to be God's marriage, which helps resolve arguments and feel loving and forgiving towards our spouse. When a marriage becomes "unbearable" couples may ask, "what is the secret to making a marriage last?" "Is it really possible to live happily ever after?" "How do I make my marriage divorce-proof?"

J. Before studying how to make your marriage endure, test your marriage. Compare your marriage to the following. Which best describes your marriage now?

1. Great joy and celebration   4. Frustration and anger
2. Busy and lacking attention   5. Infidelity and apostasy
3. Silence and unresponsive   6. Rebellion and selfishness
                                                      7. Other _____

K. Believe You are Married to the Right Person.

1. Read Genesis 21-24. When God made Eve for Adam, was she the right one for him? How did he know? How do you know you are married to the right one? __
_____
_____

2. Your mate is the right ONE for the two of you to be ONE and you believed this when you first married. When you make your commitment to them, you become the ONE. This is the one you chose from all the other ONES. To know if you married the right person is not asking yourself, "Can I picture myself with this man/woman in 50 yrs.?" Neither is it based upon time – "If we stay together for 10 years, I know I married the right person." The answer is not outside your marriage, it is within your marriage. The question now becomes "Are you learning to live with your choice?" "Are you learning to love the ONE you found?" If you do not resolve the doubt quickly, it will hang like a distant cloud on the horizon of your relationship.

3. Your mate is a gift from God and He desires your marriage to last (Ecclesiastes 9:9; Matt. 19:6).

4. If your marriage with the ONE you chose is not growing and developing as it should, it may be because you have gone against some biblical instructions. The Bible is clear. Obey God and fill your heart with certainty about your married future.

5. As God has given you this gift in the ONE you chose, He also helps sustain your marriage with the ONE. God hates divorce (Malachi 2:15,16). This is why He gives marriage what it needs to persevere. When Ecclesiastes 9:9 uses the term "labor" in association with marriage, you know WORK and TIME are part of making a marriage work. It is not an automatic success. A marriage needs nurturing, like a flower needs water, food, time, and energy.

6. It has been said, "I have married the right man/woman, because God can make me the right woman/man." In "Sacred Marriage," Gary Thomas states, "Some experts suggest it takes from 9 to 14 years for a couple to truly 'create and form its being.'" This describes a key element in the value of an enduring love and lasting marriage. It tells us many couples, who divorce within the first 5 to 6 years of marriage, never begin to experience what marriage is really like.

7. Your marriage is always taking steps of growth. Hopefully, a lot of the growth is in you personally. You married the right person. Just reconcile yourself to love him/her.

8. Becoming "one" takes TIME and WORK. It is a great adventure!

L. Be Attracted to Commitment - Promises.

1. What does Deuteronomy 23:21-23 say about commitment? _____
   _____
   _____

2. Commitment is a relationship of ONEness, not an existence. The length of marriage is not based upon how well your spouse treats you. Neither is commitment as shallow as not getting a divorce.

3. God directs your hearts in marriage (Psalm 127:1). The first thing God calls you to do is "cleave." When a marriage commits to cleave, a foundation is laid making marriage difficult to destroy (Matthew 7:24-27). The foundation of your marriage determines its length of commitment.

4. Support your promises with your ability to serve, honor, attend, share, give, and submit to one another. You made a commitment, a vow, without conditions. You committed yourself to another's care whatever the circumstance or however things might change. This is what your spouse expects. God's expectations of you are to hold to the choice you have made by fulfilling your promises. You are accountable to your spouse.

5. As a husband, who vowed to lead your wife in Christ? You would not mind someone asking, "What has God been teaching you lately?," "What are you praying about these days?," or "How is God helping you be a better husband?" (The reverse could be true for the wife.) If a wife carries a checkbook and

many "cards" in her purse, she would not mind being asked, "What did you buy today?" She would not mind her husband saying, "We need to sit down and work on our budget for the month" or "Would you please record your debit card payments."

6. Commitment does not mind advice or questions because you understand it is part of ONEness which makes an enduring marriage. Being dependable, responsible, and committed, all lead to trust, security, and safety in marriage. Romans 15:2 says, "Let each one of us please his neighbor for that which is good, unto edifying."

7. In Nehemiah 9:38, after rebuilding the walls, Israel made confession, then made a covenant with God to keep His law. The covenant was a holy arrangement, a voluntary obligation, sacred promise, and desire to follow through with their promises. Marriages need to put together and sign a marriage covenant, not a contract, to note a lifetime of fulfilling promises with love, forgiveness, and selfless spirit.

8. The decision to continue the relationship of marriage can be defined in three ways.

    a. Structural Commitment - "I Have To." There are external constraints keeping you in your marriage. "I have to stay married. I can't afford the negative consequences of divorce on my finances." "What would my friends or family say if I separated or divorced?" "Divorce would devastate my children." "My church teaches against divorce." The reason some are committed to marriage is because of prenuptial vows, money invested, children at home, church doctrine, etc.

    b. Moral Commitment - "I Ought To." "I believe staying in my marriage is the right thing to do." "I'm staying with him because of my values and beliefs." "I made a vow before God and I should keep my word." What does Romans 7:2,3 say is the responsibility we have toward marriage? _____

    _____

    God says this is an unbreakable covenant (Matthew 19:6). Every couple needs to keep this in mind to complete their marriage ('until death we do part').

    c. Personal Commitment - "I Want To." "I want to stay." "I want to continue in my marriage." "I take pleasure in being married." "I enjoy being committed to my spouse." "I enjoy being with my spouse." You love being married. You are identified as married. It is "commitment-no-matter-what." You do not balance the ledgers every month to see if you are getting an adequate return on your investment. You are here to stay. You do not get up each morning asking, "Will I stay married?" This is called intentional marriage. Gary Chapman said it is "living the love you promised."

9. STORY: "In Thornton Wilder's 'The Skin of Our Teeth,' a character named Ms. Antobus says, "I married you because you gave me a promise. That promise made up for your faults. And the promise I gave you made up for mine. Two

imperfect people got married and it was the promise that made the marriage. And when our children were growing up, it wasn't a house that protected them; and it wasn't our love that protected them — it was that promise.' That's a great example of what a commitment to marriage looks like. It's a promise made and kept by two imperfect people — with flaws, faults, and character weaknesses" ("One Marriage Under God," H. Norman Wright).

10. The model of a committed marriage is doing what you promised (Ecclesiastes 5:2-5) without having conditions to be met. (EX.: her to respect me first, him to show me affection first, her to admire me, him to say "I'm sorry," etc). None of these stipulations were in the vows. God holds you to the promise and so does your spouse.

11. The model of a committed marriage is understanding the unknown of the future (car wreck, disease, childlessness, cancer, etc.). It is persevering in spite of the failures of our mate. It is much like what Jesus said in Luke 9:62 about being a disciple, once started, do not look back.

12. The model of a committed marriage is like God's perseverance with Israel. There were days of victory, celebration, joy, infidelity, frustration, anger, disappointment, return, forgiveness, etc. and God did not turn His back. God says, "I will never leave thee" (Hebrews 13:5). This is a model all marriages need to imitate. God's love for us is enduring (Romans 5:8). It does not decrease over time.

13. STORY: An older couple was discussing their upcoming 50th anniversary in the grocery checkout line. The young cashier interjected, "I can't imagine being married to the same man for 50 years!" The wife wisely replied, "Well, honey, don't get married until you can!"

14. Never threaten to leave. Divorce is not an option. Do not joke about it or even think about it.

15. Real men and women stay faithful. They do not have time to look for another because they are busy seeking new ways to love their own.

16. Living in a nation of quitters and unfaithfulness, what do YOU believe is essential to keep YOUR commitment to YOUR marriage and make for an enduring marriage? _____

_____

17. If both or one of you gave up on your marriage, what would be lost? _____

_____

_____

_____

18. Look through the scriptures. What Bible person or people illustrate the character of perseverance? How could their example help you with endurance in your marriage? _____

_____

_____

M. Maintain Purity In Your Marriage.

1. Read 1 Thessalonians 4:1-6. What does this say about purity? _____
   _____
   _____

2. Purity is not just a possession you bring into your marriage and keep in marriage. The need for purity does not stop after marriage. You really need to hold it MORE and LONGER!

3. Read Ephesians 5:25-27. From this text, what should be the characteristic of the church? _____
   _____

   How is this parallel with marriage? _____
   _____

4. Establish boundaries to have a pure marriage. When scripture says a wife "is bound by the law to the husband while he *liveth*" (Romans 7:2), it does not only tell you how long your relationship lasts, it establishes the boundary as to whom you are bound.

5. The boundaries which protect your marriage are like "invisible fences", keeping you restrained for your own protection and safety morally, emotionally, physically, and spiritually. Boundaries keep a marriage on sacred ground with your mate.

6. Protect your marriage by reminding yourself of your love for your spouse. A book entitled "Hedges" by Jerry Jenkins (1990) says the greatest gift you can give your spouse is to set up some boundaries with members of the opposite sex including, but not limited to: avoid flirting, do not be alone behind closed doors with a member of the opposite sex, and monitor what you watch. In Job 31:1, Job said, "I made a covenant with my eyes not to look lustfully at a girl."

7. A husband keeps his marriage pure by being intoxicated with the love of one woman. Be the leader of one woman. Establish boundaries with your eyes (Proverbs 4:20-26). Place a boundary on the internet, TV, or whatever engages you and draws you away from being the husband your wife needs. Escape with your wife, not with a mouse click or remote control. Read Proverbs 5:15-20. What exhortations does this passage give a husband?
   _____

   A husband brings safety, security, refuge, defense, and protection to his marriage when he understands the power of his eyes. Look deep into the eyes of your mate.

8. A wife keeps her marriage pure being intoxicated with one man. Respect, admire, and be attracted to the leading of one man. A wife understands the power of her body and establishes boundaries with what she wears. What wisdom can a wife find in 1 Timothy 2:9,10 and 1 Peter 3:3,4 about the way she adorns herself in marriage? _____
   _____
   _____

9. Have boundaries with what you wear regardless of the season. Do not become the window dressing for another man's eyes. Why wear something and defraud another man of something he cannot have. What does 1 Thessalonians 5:4 say helps a woman maintain purity with her body? _____
_____
_____

N. Speak to the Heart of Your Spouse.

1. Read Deuteronomy 6:1-6. What did God hope Israel would learn each day?
_____
_____

2. The above example shows how important it was to communicate with the heart of the Israelites. God would not communicate once, then let them go. He would not speak to them only when times were difficult or enemies came close, but always.

3. God knew the value of speaking to Israel. So, each spouse in marriage should also. What was the last thing you said to your spouse this morning before leaving? Did you speak to the heart of your spouse? _____
_____

4. Communication is the "lifeblood of marriage." Take it away and your marriage fails.

5. Romans 12:15 shows the importance of understanding the heart of others. Speak to your spouse's heart by being transparent. Although it creates risks by revealing your deep thoughts, ideas, fears, needs, concerns, hopes, and dreams, you protect your marriage. The word has power to know what is in your heart (Hebrews 4:12). Does your spouse have access to yours?

6. Give your spouse words of encouragement every day. Honor, motivate, and speak about your mate's spiritual gifts and natural talents. Discover the weaknesses and fears with which your spouse struggles. Why is this so important? Your spouse has an intimate need for acceptance, affection, appreciation, approval, attention, comfort, encouragement, respect, security, and support. Who can give this the best —YOU!

7. One of the greatest ways to speak to your spouse's heart is to pursue his/her voice.

8. Don't take your spouse for granted. Everyday tell your mate something you appreciate about her/him and how grateful you are to have them in your life.

9. Continue dating your spouse.

O. Be a Life Long Learner.

1. Read 1 Peter 3:7. What responsibility is expressed in this passage? _____
   _____
   _____

2. List the top 5 needs of your spouse? Is your list based on what you assume are their needs or what you know are their needs? _____
   _____
   _____
   _____
   _____

3. Here is a revelation. The needs of your spouse are not the same at 20, 30, or 40 years into your marriage as they were 5 days into your marriage.

4. Your marriage lasts by spending your life learning about your spouse. Read Hebrews 5:12-14. Some couples, like Christians, need to be taught again how to be husbands and wives. Some never learn. Some do not want to know. Some older couples should be teaching other couples, but cannot because they need teaching again. Some older couples 15, 20, and 40 years into marriage never knew how to lead, submit, love, and provide. One man in Christ in his 70's said to us, "I don't want people following my marriage."

5. As 2 Peter 3:18 says, "grow in the grace and knowledge of our Lord and Saviour." Let your marriage grow by learning more from God about what you need to be. Be teachable. You never reach the point where you know all there is about marriage. Let God create in you His workmanship (Ephesians 2:10; 4:24). You will never be the husband or wife your spouse needs you to be unless you take responsibility to cultivate your spiritual life. As your spouse sees and hears your learning, they will accept you more, rather than reject you.

6. Many couples have yet to discover the secret to a lasting marriage, learning to serve their spouse (Matthew 20:28; Philippians 2:3,4). Before Ephesians 5:22-33 speaks about the parallel of Christ and the church to marriage, v.21 sets the tone for the discussion, "submitting to one another in the fear of Christ." What my mate needs is more important than what I need. This means there are attitudes to be discarded and adjustments to be made to become a servant in the marriage. If you do not know the ways to serve your spouse, ask her/him what they need from you. "Walk in your spouse's shoes." Minister to them (Galatians 6:2; Romans 15:1-4). Getting intimately involved in your spouse's life is not meant to please you, but to please the other. In other words, a marriage does not last with selfishness.

7. If you want to learn to be a better husband, read and study Ephesians 5:23-33, and a wife should study Proverbs 31:10-31. The endurance of your marriage is knowing your responsibilities to your mate. If you stop learning, you stop giving. Ask God for wisdom in how to be a better servant.

8. Read Ephesians 5:15,16. Being a lifelong learner takes TIME. Provide yourself TIME to practice what you learn. Unless you purposefully protect time, all of life's little "urgent" needs will undermine your marital intimacy like termites, slowly eat away the foundation of a house. More men take time to know how to run a business than lead a marriage. More women take time to know more about their children than they do their husbands. WHY? Men worship their jobs. Women worship their children. What can be more urgent than protecting your marriage by learning what to do for your spouse?

P. Have an Intentional Marriage.

1. If there is no purpose, the future of your marriage is in jeopardy (Proverbs 29:18).

2. No marriage runs on autopilot, thinking it will last forever.

3. Unless you become intentional in marriage, you will borrow time from your spouse and put it toward hobbies, work, children, civic clubs, sports, etc. Being intentional in marriage needs to be intense in the face of distractions.

4. Both husband and wife need to think about their relationship, plan for their relationship, and act for their relationship in practical simple ways in order to have and maintain connection.

5. Intend for it to reflect the image of God (Genesis 2:22-25; Ephesians 5:1,2). Let it be a picture of Christ's commitment and love for the church (Ephesians 5:22-31).

6. You can be intentional in marriage through...

   a. Having rituals in your marriage. Certain things need repetition (saying "I Love You," giving a card, gift, flowers, etc. for anniversary, go on a boat ride Labor Day weekend, daily shoulder rub, "trademarks," 3rd Friday night of the month, etc.). Repetition boosts your marriage commitment. This is something emotionally special.

   b. Daily time together. Pick a time for "us" time. Do not worry about the length of time, just have a beginning time to focus on each other. Pick a place you will always go (dinner table, couch, porch swing, sitting at the foot of the bed, etc.)

   c. Being open and honest. Being naked emotionally and not ashamed (Genesis 2:25) is a missing link for a lasting marriage. Couples, who take conflicts, mistakes, disappointments, difficulties, and other unfulfilled expectations and confront their differences, will pray, confess, adjust, and forgive. Control your emotions. Honestly appreciate the differences each of you have.

   d. Having an eternal view of your marriage (Romans 2:7,8). Each spouse needs to have eternity in their hearts (Ecclesiastes 3:11). This means having a spiritual mind focused on the ways of the Father. Unless you and your spouse are spiritually connected, your marriage will lack understanding of how a marriage begins, lives, and ends. Spirituality in marriage cuts the likelihood of divorce by 30-35% (University of Virginia study: Brad Wilcox and another study by Annette Mahoney, Bowling Green University). Have holiness in your marriage!

Q. Some people have said regarding their marriage, "It's too late for me...," "I have nothing left in marriage worth keeping." "There is no hope for us." While you have your mate, it is not too late. We have a God of hope, help, and healing. The door is still open. You marriage does not have to "survive." It can be "revived."

R. EX: A couple who had isolated themselves from one another gave their marriage one more chance. They started over. They put time and work into their marriage. They had a baby girl and named her HOPE because God had revived their marriage and created holiness and righteousness in their marriage in the same way He does all those who "put off the old man" and "put on the new man." It is never too late to start doing what is right with your marriage.

S. 1 Corinthians 13:8 says, love "beareth all things, believeth all things, hopeth all things, endureth all things. Love never faileth." How does love help a spouse stay true to their mate as long "as they both shall live?" _____
_____
_____

T. If you were advising a couple to "stick with it," what would you say to them? _____
_____
_____

U. Image Builders for Your Marriage.

1. Develop a commitment covenant for your marriage. Write down what is needed in your marriage to make it last. Both spouses sign the covenant.

2. Discuss together the scripture that outlines your strategy for an enduring marriage? Print it out and keep it with you always.

3. Write a love letter to each other once every two to three years stating why you married your spouse. Include the qualities which drew you to him/her (i.e. love for God, honesty, support, respect, sacrifice, time, kindness, leader, affection, etc.). In your letter, remind him/her of your commitment to them regardless. Find a special place to share these letters with each other. Let this be your "special spot."

4. Start and continue showing public expressions of affection.

5. Understand what prayer does in your marriage. Have a special prayer together EVERY day. It reminds you of who really is the Source of strength in your marriage. It keeps you connected and communicating with your spouse.

6. Read the book "Five Love Languages" by Gary Smalley. Learn how to speak to your spouse's heart.

7. Let the thoughts of Philippians 4:8 be applied to your marriage. To start with, for the next 30 days, do not say anything negative about your spouse to him/her or others. Find something you appreciate about your spouse and verbalize it. This has the power to transform a marriage. When you examine and work to change yourself, you often find yourself bringing out the best in your spouse as well.

8. Take this self-evaluation test of your marriage to see if you believe your marriage will endure.

   a. Have you or do you ever threaten to leave your spouse?

   b. Are you or your mate secure in your commitment to your marriage?

   c. Are you more committed to your mate than to your career?

   d. Are you more committed to your mate than to your children?

   e. Are you more committed to your mate than to your hobbies and favorite activities?

   f. Do you emotionally leave your mate by withdrawing for an extended period of time because of conflict?

   g. Are you interested in meeting your mate's needs and actively pursuing what you can to meet them?

   h. Would you marry your spouse again, although they may not be lovable or loving? Do you really love her/him?

   i. After answering these questions, write out how you plan to demonstrate commitment to your spouse in the next five years. Ask God to give you courage to fulfill your commitment, even if your spouse does not respond.

9. Keep yourself mentally and physically in shape. Change your attitudes and behaviors when necessary. Take self care by reducing stress, eating healthy, and exercising. A lasting marriage needs energy. Follow a program to keep your health in order to enjoy a "growing old together" marriage (1 Corinthians 6:19,20).

10. Develop common interests you can share together. Talk about and develop new interests.

11. Finish the race together (Philippians 3:12-16; Hebrews 12:2).

12. Decide every day to make your marriage last.

13. What will your children say you believe about marriage?

35 Lessons From 35 Years Of Marriage

❧ Marriage is about reflecting the image of God.

❧ Spiritual intimacy is the number one intimacy above sexual, emotional, and social intimacy.

❧ Marriage is a world of discovery at any stage from newlywed to the golden years.

❧ Romance is not just for holidays. It is for every day.

❧ Your words are seeds sown in the heart of your spouse for bad or good. In time, you will reap thorns or flowers.

❧ Saying, "I Need You," to your spouse provides marriage security, trust, and commitment.

❧ Your spouse is not your enemy - Satan is.

❧ Praying together means your marriage stays together.

❧ Keep humility in your marriage. Your marriage is not guaranteed to last a lifetime.

❧ Build your marriage on the Rock, not the world. When the storm comes, your marriage remains intact.

❧ Husbands and wives will always think differently, and there is nothing wrong with this.

❧ Ephesians 4 is the best chapter on communication. Read it often. Apply its thoughts.

❧ Unless you have a vision for your marriage, it will never be better than what it is now.

❧ Your marriage is what your children believe marriage will be for them.

❧ Spiritual leadership is the greatest need of a wife. Respect is the greatest need of a husband.

❧ Romance gave you children, but do not let your children steal your romance.

❧ Purity is not only something you practice before marriage. You need it in marriage.

❧ Whatever won your spouse over to you, keep doing it. It never gets old.

❧ Romance to a husband is spelled S-E-X. Romance to a wife is spelled C-O-N-N-E-C-T-I-O-N.

❧ Determine what your values are and read off the same blueprint as you raise your children.

❧ Teach your son to be a man, God's man. Teach your daughter to be a woman, God's woman.

❧ Sexual intimacy is beautiful at any age. Honor it in your heart. Your bed is "holy ground".

ಬ Love is a choice, not a feeling. Marriage needs a love like 1 Corinthians 13. Work the list.

ಬ Be attentive to your spouse's needs. Check on what you can do for him/her.

ಬ The greatest threat to your marriage is loneliness. Never isolate yourself from your mate. Be ONE.

ಬ Every couple needs a mentoring couple who is one season of life ahead of them.

ಬ Marriage is the union of two imperfect people who need mercy, where confession is freely asked for, and forgiveness is given without criticism or holding a grudge.

ಬ A husband needs to act like a man and lead. A wife needs to act like a woman and submit.

ಬ BUSYNESS takes a marriage and destroys it one second at a time.

ಬ Never take your spouse for granted. Your mate likes to hear "thank you" as much as anyone.

ಬ Every day believe you are married to the right person – the ONE.

ಬ Be a life-long learner. Have a teachable spirit. There is always something to learn about marriage.

ಬ Be a servant. Do not always wind up on the receiving end of your mate's kindness.

ಬ Build your marriage to outlast your children when they leave home.

ಬ "Except the Lord build the house, they labor in vain that build it," - Psalm 127:1.

What Makes A Marriage Last

IT'S THE EVERYDAY CHOICES YOU MAKE:

To do what is best for your partner in life...

To respect the commitment of being husband and wife...

To be still and just listen—not have to be heard...

To forgive and forget and not need "the last word"...

To admit you're not perfect—you'll both make mistakes...

To support the decisions that each of you makes...

To be willing to laugh when a day has been rough...

To divide up the burdens when life becomes tough...

To support one another when things are too hurried...

To comfort each other when stress keeps you worried...

To be willing to cherish your true love and friend

with a joy and compassion that will never end.

As You celebrate each year together:

May you always have understanding to make your marriage work,

Commitment to make your marriage grow

And love to make your marriage happy!

(Author Unknown)

Thirty Ways To Spiritually Lead Your Wife

1. Believe, accept, and commit to the role God gave you as a man, a husband, and as a father.
2. Pray daily with her.
3. Write a love letter that she would like to receive.
4. Discover her top 3 needs and over the next 12 months go all out to meet them.
5. Buy her a rose. Take her in your arms. Hold her face gently. Look into her eyes and say, "I'd marry you all over again!"
6. Hold her hand and tell her how glad you are God made her for you.
7. Read the scriptures to her.
8. Use ONLY the "C" word—commitment. Never the "D" word—divorce.
9. Live with her in an understanding way (1 Peter 3:7).
10. Remain faithful to her.
11. Fulfill your marriage covenant.
12. Have a family time at least one night a week.
13. Protect your wife's modesty. Keep her pure in the public eye. Objectively judge her clothes before she leaves the house. Let her demonstrate godliness.
14. Protect your marriage from evil.
15. Learn to make righteous judgments.
16. Set spiritual goals for your children.
17. Remember to praise your wife's strengths and pray for her weaknesses.
18. Protect your wife from false teaching.
19. Protect your wife from the immoral things of this world.
20. Do a Proverbs breakfast or supper Bible study.
21. Hug and Kiss your wife and children every day.
22. Ask your wife for forgiveness when you fail her and your family. Give her mercy when she needs it.
23. Have a vision for your marriage (Proverbs 29:18). Develop a mission statement to describe your marriage and family.
24. Call your wife and children to a spiritual mission to do what God wants to do with their life.
25. Persevere and do not quit.
26. Talk to God and let God talk to you about leading your marriage.
27. Do not surrender your love for your wife for the admiration of another woman.
28. Surrender to Jesus.
29. Ask your wife to pray for you to accept the role of leadership.
30. Be strong. Do not be afraid. Have courage. Obey the law of God as God told Joshua (Joshua 1:7-9).

101 Ways to Tell Your Wife "I Love You"

1. LEAVE CANDY FOR HER TO FIND And I'm not talking about a 3 Musketeers bar. (Unless that's what she likes). Buy a pretty box of chocolates. Leave them in her car or some other place that she's sure to find them. Tuck a little "I love you" note inside to increase the effect.

2. DO NOT TEASE HER FOR PRIMPING She wants to look nice for you! If you constantly go on about how much time she spends on her hair or manicures, she may take it that you don't appreciate her femininity or her effort to look pretty. Let her know she's beautiful when she takes time to primp.

3. KISS HER FOR AT LEAST 6 SECONDS Forget the little peck on your way out the door in the morning. Give her a kiss that will stay with her all day! Kissing for at least six seconds doesn't take that long but it makes for a much more meaningful kiss.

4. HOLD HANDS Wives feel special when their husbands reach over and take their hand. It's just a simple gesture, but it goes a long way.

5. MAIL HER A LETTER E-mail has its place, but for a woman, getting a letter in the mailbox addressed to her from her hubby...well now, that's just too romantic!

6. LEAVE HER A TIP You'll leave the waitress a tip, but what about the lady who is there to wait on you 24/7? Surprise her as she clears the supper table; leave her a few dollars to show your appreciation.

7. REENACT YOUR FIRST DATE Tell your wife that you're taking her out. Tell her that you think it would be fun to do everything just like you did on your first date then try to reenact it! The bonus is that you won't have to take her home to her father, you can take her home with you!

8. DEDICATE A SONG TO HER Call your local radio station and have them to play a song for your sweetie! Tell them why you love her and her name, and have them to repeat it over the air!

9. COMMUNICATE WITH HER Your wife wants in on your life. Tell her about your day or even your hopes and dreams for the future. Talk about the kids, or whatever happens to come to mind. Just communicate!

10. WHISPER IN HER EAR Get close to your wife and whisper those sweet words of love in her ear. Try whispering something about your private love life in the middle of a public place and watch her blush!

11. HAVE FLOWERS DELIVERED TO HER Take some time out of your lunch break to swing by the flower shop. Have the florist deliver her flowers to your home or at her place of work, or deliver them yourself!

12. PUT YOUR ARM AROUND HER Put your arm around your wife while she's sitting next to you or while walking side by side.

13. CARESS HER Gently caress your wife's hair with your hand or her face with your lips. She loves to feel your touch.

14. PRAISE HER IN FRONT OF OTHERS Let your wife hear you brag on her while you're talking to others. She may blush or say something back, but secretly she's feeling proud that you're her man.

15. PRAISE HER TO HER FACE Tell your wife that you appreciate all that she does and the love that she shows to you.

16. TAKE HER ON A SURPRISE DATE Secretly arrange for someone to watch your children, if you have them, then surprise your wife by taking her out for a night that she'll not soon forget!

17. LEAVE THE STRESS OF WORK AT WORK I'm not saying that you can't talk to your wife about your job or the things that bother you. I'm saying that if you've had a bad day, don't take it out on your wife and family. It's easy to be grumpy after a long day of work. Don't snap at the people who love you. If you need to vent your frustrations, talk them out with your wife. She'll be glad to lend an ear if you need to talk.

18. DO NOT HIDE ANYTHING FROM YOUR WIFE Be open and honest with your wife about everything. Keep an open line of communication between the two of you at all times. Keeping things from her, even small things, can hurt a relationship. If she should find out from another source, she would feel hurt and disappointed that you didn't feel like you could share with her. This could ultimately damage her trust in you as well.

19. TAKE CARE OF THE CARS Make sure that your vehicles are in tip top shape at all times so your wife isn't left stranded. Don't expect her to go to the dirty garages to get the oil changed and repairs done, do them yourself, or take them in for her.

20. COMPLIMENT HER Everyone needs a compliment now and then, but many wives need a little extra reassurance to make sure that she's still special in your eyes. A compliment doesn't cost you anything, but for your wife, it is priceless!

21. BUY HER A FEMININE GIFT Buy your wife a gift that makes her feel feminine, like her favorite perfume, or lingerie.

22. DO NOT FORGET SPECIAL OCCASIONS Put it on your phone schedule, hang a calendar in your vehicle, do what you must, but DON'T forget your anniversary, her birthday, or Valentine's Day!

23. ALWAYS KISS HER GOODNIGHT Never even close your eyes at night until you've kissed your wife goodnight. (For at least 6 seconds).

24. FINISH HOME IMPROVEMENT PROJECTS Too many times husbands work so hard all week that they don't feel like keeping up the repairs at home. This is understandable, but remember, it often makes your wife's work harder too. If you work on things for just awhile, and aim to finish at least one project per month, it makes your whole household run smoother.

25. DO NOT BE NEGATIVE Don't go around griping or nitpicking the things your wife does or doesn't do. Try to be more pleasant. Look on the positive side of things. When you are negative, it makes everything look worse than it really is.

26. TAKE A SHOWER TOGETHER Here's a way to get clean and have fun at the same time! Jump in the shower, mesh together, and do a lot of kissing! Be sensitive if your wife feels insecure, and make sure that you reassure her often.

27. SHOW PATIENCE DURING HORMONAL TIMES If your wife gets a little difficult to live with during certain times of the month, be patient. This is especially important too if she's pregnant or a new mother. She can't control her emotions very well during these times, and will need your support.

28. ADMIT IT WHEN YOU'RE WRONG If you are in the wrong, admit it. Don't pass it off like it's no big deal, or make excuses for yourself. You're not too macho to say, "I'm sorry" if you're in the wrong. In fact you'll be a much bigger man if you do.

29. LOOK INTO HER EYES While talking to or hugging your wife, look her straight in the eyes while cupping her face in your hand. She may feel shy and try to look away, but don't confuse this with thinking she doesn't like it. Gently insist she look at you, then slowly lean down and kiss her. (For at least 6 seconds).

30. SACRIFICE FOR HER Put aside something that you want so that you can give something to your wife. Usually, this is what wives do. They'll put aside their own needs to make sure their family gets everything they need first. Make sure your wife is taking good care of herself too.

31. WRITE HER A LOVE POEM Put your romantic thoughts into a rhyme that your wife will cherish forever! Not a poet? Just write down your feelings the best you can, she'll love it!

32. GIVE HER A MASSAGE Grab the oil and lotion, then grab your wife! Give her a full body massage and help her relax. (Try to at least get past her shoulders before moving on to "other things)."

33. PLAY A GAME TOGETHER Bring out the board games or play a game of tennis. Playing a game together can help keep the two of you close. If she beats you, admit it. Don't say, "Oh, I just let you win."

34. CALL IF YOU'RE GOING TO BE LATE Don't make your wife worry about you, or let dinner get cold. Take 5 minutes to phone her if you see you're going to be late.

35. WASH THE DISHES FOR HER You don't have to clean the whole house, but just doing one chore such as the dishes once in a while, or at least cleaning up after yourself, will help her out a lot.

36. PICK HER FLOWERS OK, you've sent her flowers, but why not pick some wildflowers yourself? Stop the car and pick some by the roadside, then gently tuck one behind your wife's ear and kiss her neck.

37. TAKE HER TO A ROMANTIC PLAY Skip the movie and head out to a theatrical play. If there's not a good romantic one showing, find one with some good, clean humor.

38. PLAY A KISSING GAME Lock lips and see who can hold out the longest!

39. GIVE HER A NIGHT OFF Watch the kids while she heads out to shop for awhile. Throw in a few extra bucks so that she can buy herself something special.

40. DO NOT MENTION HER WEIGHT No matter what size your wife may be, discussing her weight is definitely a "no, no."

41. DO NOT ARGUE OVER FINANCES If money gets tight, be very careful not to argue or shift blame. Together, and in a business-like fashion, explore ways that you can pay off your debts. If things spin out of control, consider financial counseling. Your marriage is worth more than money.

42. LEAVE LOVE NOTES IN UNEXPECTED PLACES Try leaving love notes in odd places that she'll be sure to see, such as under windshield wipers, inside the

refrigerator, inside a CD case or even on toilet paper! A good example would be to put one on the light switch that says, "You turn me on."

43. BE HONEST NEVER EVER lie to your wife, even if it seems harmless. Trust is one of the most important factors in a marriage - don't break it!

44. RENEW YOUR WEDDING VOWS Although we know that the first vows are good for life, still, taking your wife to a chapel on your anniversary, or any day, and renewing your vows lets her know that you'd marry her all over again.

45. WORSHIP TOGETHER Find time to worship and pray with your wife. Our lives our made up of three parts. Body, mind, and spirit. You need to connect in all three ways to be close.

46. RESPECT HER Showing respect is another important factor in a marriage. Don't degrade her, yell at her, or misuse her.

47. PROVIDE FOR HER Do your best to provide for your wife and family. You don't have to buy a castle, just make sure it's nice and comfortable and there's food on the table. If your wife chooses to help out that's OK, but it is your place to provide, so don't expect her to fill that role.

48. TELL HER YOU NEED HER Let her know that your life just wouldn't be complete if you didn't have her. Tell her that you not only want her in your life, but that you need her.

49. LET HER CRY Every woman needs a good cry now and then; sometimes she can tell you why, and sometimes she can't. Just make sure you don't get irritated at her or make fun of her. This makes everything worse. Take her in your arms and hold her until everything is better. This may be the very thing she needed anyway.

50. DO NOT TEASE HER TOO MUCH It's OK to tease now and then, but try to keep it at a minimum. Don't excessively tease her in front of others, and never tease in a degrading fashion.

51. DO NOT CORRECT HER IN FRONT OF OTHERS If you feel that your wife has been a little out of line or has done something that you disapprove of, it's OK to talk it over with her in private, but never jump her in front of others; especially your children. Make sure you are loving even if you're firm.

52. BE FAITHFUL Always make sure that you're faithful to your wife in every angle. Keep your body, your eyes, and your thoughts only for her. If you are facing any temptation, remove yourself from the source. Be open with your wife about your needs so that she can be the one to fill them.

53. GIVE HER LOTS OF CUDDLE TIME Wives like to be cuddled and kissed without sex sometimes. Try sitting in front of a campfire or laying under the stars and just take your time.

54. LISTEN Sometimes wives just need to talk - about anything. Show interest and listen to her when she talks. If she's upset, show concern. If she's happy, laugh with her. Try to pick up on clues that she may be dropping in her conversation to let you know her needs.

55. BE FORGIVING If your wife does something that offends you, be quick to forgive. Holding hard feelings ruins a marriage. Let her know in a heartfelt way how she made you feel, then let it go.

56. BE THE LEADER OF YOUR HOME Many wives don't want their husbands to be the leader because they dominate. But if you're a good leader, you will also serve. Home leadership is meant to be the husbands role, and if done it right, it takes an unnecessary load off of your wife. Set reasonable guidelines and goals for your household. Ask your wife for advice too. Sometimes a woman sees things not only in the practical sense, like most men do, but she also uses her heart to even things out.

57. BE CLEAN AND NEAT Keep yourself groomed, clean, and smelling nice.

58. PROVIDE SECURITY Let your wife feel secure in your love without worrying if you will still love her from day to day.

59. FIND OUT WHAT HER NEEDS ARE SEXUALLY Your wife's sexual needs sometimes vary a great deal from yours. Find out how and where she likes to be touched, and what she expects from sex, and try to fill her needs.

60. HELP OUT WHEN SHE DOESN'T FEEL WELL If your wife is sick or has had a bad day, try helping with her household duties and with the kids. Make sure she gets plenty of rest.

61. DON'T COMPARE HER IN A NEGATIVE WAY Don't say things like, "You gripe just like your Aunt Thelma." Comparison often hurts self esteem.

62. TAKE HER ON WEEKEND TRIPS Take your wife to a romantic resort for the weekend. If your budget's a little tight, consider checking into a hotel, even if it's local, so the two of you can get away from the familiar and just enjoy each other.

63. BE VERBAL WHEN MAKING LOVE When making love, describe aloud and in detail each thing that you do and how it makes you feel. This arouses your wife. Let her know that she's meeting your needs as well.

64. SHOP FOR A GIFT TO SHARE Go shopping for something that you'll both enjoy together. Get a great CD, massage oils, or anything that you'll both like.

65. ENCOURAGE HER TO FOLLOW HER DREAMS If your wife has dreams and goals that she would like to accomplish, be her best cheer leader. Support her as she endeavors to reach them.

66. BE KIND AND COURTEOUS Treat your wife as you would expect her to treat you. Treat her with dignity and be courteous at all times.

67. DO NOT DO ANNOYING THINGS If you must pass gas, go to the bathroom. Don't do it to annoy her, or burp at the table. It's not as funny as you think it is - as a matter of fact, it's not funny at all.

68. FLIRT WITH YOUR WIFE Don't stop flirting with her just because you're married. Do it now more than ever to keep that spark! Wink at her from across the room, whistle at her, or give her "that look." Watch her cheeks turn rosy.

69. TAKE A JACUZZI BATH TOGETHER Jacuzzis are one of the world's most romantic inventions! Some use it for stress, some use it for... If you don't have a jacuzzi tub, check into a hotel that has a tub for two, and spend the night.

70. TAKE A WALK Go for a long walk through a park or take a moonlight stroll. Hold hands while you walk.

71. LOOK OUT FOR THE FUTURE You plan on being together for life, right? Make sure that your future will be secure. Set up a retirement fund. Also, although no one wants to think about it, we all will die one day. Take out a life insurance policy to make sure that if the worst should happen, your family will be cared for.

72. SET UP A SLIDE SHOW Pick out special photo memories from the time that you were dating to the present. Create a slide show with music. This is something that you can do together and can help keep you close.

73. DO NOT RUSH SEX While the two of you are in the middle of the wonderful marital gift of sex, be careful not to rush it. Let your wife know that you're loving her, not just the moment.

74. DO NOT BELITTLE HER OPINIONS If your wife has an opinion or an idea, thank her, and let her know that her thoughts are valuable. Don't act like her ideas are unintelligent or crazy.

75. CHERISH HER DIFFERENCES Your wife has a different make up than you and it shows in more ways than one. Not only in her body, but the way she thinks and receives love are naturally "different." Cherish these differences and don't try to change her.

76. BE DEVOTED TO HER HAPPINESS Do what you can to make your wife happy. You don't have to buy her the most expensive things or "spoil" her rotten, (though that's OK too). Usually a little goes a long way for most wives, and just giving a little attention now and then makes her feel loved and appreciated. You will find that if she's happy, she'll respond better to your needs as well.

77. REMINISCE YOUR WEDDING NIGHT Women like to remember special times. Bring up your wedding night and how it felt to have sex for the first time. Talk about your high school graduations or the day your kids were born.

78. MAKE HER LATE FOR BREAKFAST Wake her up by kissing her! Not only is this a pleasant way to wake, but she might keep you there through breakfast!

79. MAKE A JOURNAL Start on her birthday or Christmas and write a love note or something special to your wife everyday for a year. At the end of the year, present it to her as a gift.

80. GIVE HER A NICKNAME Give her your own special name, like "Beautiful" or "Angel."

81. HAVE YOUR PHOTO MADE WITH HER Go have a professional, up-to-date photo done of the two of you. Try romantic scenes such as a park or waterfall.

82. GO ON A SECOND HONEYMOON Remember how special your honeymoon was? Take another one, and try to make it better than the first.

83. START A HOBBY TOGETHER Find a hobby that you both enjoy, such as horse back riding or tennis. Do it together as often as you can to help stay close.

84. HELP HER DRESS OR UNDRESS Help your wife with the buttons or snaps. Caress her gently as you help her put on or take off her clothes. When taking off her clothes, do it slowly, piece by piece.

85. SHOW HUMILITY Don't get a big head and think that you can't be touched with a ten foot pole. You wife wants you to be confident, but don't think that you're the master of all.

86. PROTECT HER Look after your wife making sure that she's not in any situations where she could be harmed physically or emotionally. This includes verbal abuse from cantankerous family members. Always be quick to stand up for her in any given situation.

87. BE HER BEST FRIEND Be there for your wife at all times and in every situation. Let her feel confident enough to share anything with you.

88. BE THE CHEF Cook up a romantic meal for your wife. Even if you're not a cook, you can find something that you can make. Just follow the box or cookbook directions. Macaroni and cheese can be romantic if it comes from your heart. Just set the table with some candles and turn out the lights. What could be more romantic than eating macaroni and cheese in candlelight with an adoring husband who's tried so hard to please you?

89. GET RID OF IRRITATING HABITS Do you have a habit that bugs your wife? Try to take the necessary measures to stop it.

90. PLANT A GARDEN TOGETHER Whether it's a flower garden or a vegetable garden, growing things takes lots of work. Why not do it together? This cuts the work in half, and is a great way to enjoy each other's company. Then when it's all said and done, enjoy the fruits of your labor by picking and eating the veggies, or decorating the table with the lovely flowers.

91. BUY A SEASON PASS Buy season passes to the zoo or a museum. The cost comes once a year, so if you're a little tight on money at some point, you always have a place to go.

92. DO NOT BE A WORKAHOLIC!(Or any other kind of "holic" for that matter). Make sure there is always time to spend with your wife and family. In a few years, the money won't matter anyway, and you just have one chance at life. Make the most of it with the ones you love; don't live with regrets.

93. MAKE A LIST OF LOVE Make a list of every reason that you love your wife and post it on the refrigerator.

94. SPEAK IN YOUR OWN CODE Create a secret code word for something that only the two of you know, and say it openly in public! It's like having your own secret language!

95. NIBBLE Pull your wife close and nibble her ear or lips. This gives her cold chills!

96. GRAB A KISS WHILE WAITING. If you're at a stop light or in a long line at the drive-through, pull your wife close and grab a kiss. (Remember, at least six seconds, although you may want to go longer)!

97. TELL THE WORLD HOW MUCH YOU LOVE HER. Put a bumper sticker on your vehicle that says, "I Love My Wife," or put up a sign in your yard that says, "The Prettiest Lady In the World Lives Here."

98. JUST SAY THE WORDS. Tell your wife everyday, several times a day, that you love her.

99. PRACTICE ALL THE CHARACTERISTICS OF LOVE IN 1 CORINTHIANS 13. Let these words be displayed in you as her husband. She will mimic them back to you in ways your marriage will appreciate.

100.   ACCEPT HER THE WAY SHE IS. Give yourself the opportunity to discover something new about your wife. There is always something unique about her that makes her special to you.

101.   FORGIVE HER AS YOU WOULD WANT HER TO FORGIVE YOU. She needs your mercy to bring you closer to her and to God. Your intimacy with God depends on His mercy. Your intimacy with your wife depends on the mercy you extend to her (Matthew 6:14,15).

References

- Divorce's Guide to Marriage, by Elizabeth Bernstein, http://online.wsj.com/article/SB10000 872396390444025204577544951717564114.html.
- Devotions for Sacred Marriage, by Gary Thomas.
- 10 Principles to Keep Christ at the Center of Your Home, by Mary My Larmoyeux http://www.familylife.com/articles/topics/marriage/staying-married/growing-spiritually/10-principles-to-keep-christ-at-the-center-of-your-home.
- Do You Really Need Your Spouse, by Dennis Rainey http://www.familylife.com/articles/topics/marriage/staying-married/communication/do-you-really-need-your-spouse#.UvlxA2JdWSo.
- His Needs, Her Needs, by Willard Harley.
- Three Steps to Leadership by Bob Lepine, http://www.familylife.com/articles/topics/marriage/staying-married/husbands/3-steps-to-leadership#.Uvlx4GJdWSo.
- Time Bandits—A Conversation with Les and Leslie Parrott, http://www.growthtrac.com/artman/publish/a-conversation-with-les-leslie-parrott-1038.php#ixzz1jHSqodMw.
- The Pressure Test, by Dennis and Barbara Rainey, http://mentor.gofamilylife.com/2011/07/the-pressure-test/.
- Fight Fair, by Tim and Joy Downs.
- Staying Close, by Dennis and Barbara Rainey.
- Family Life Today, http://www.familylife.com/.
- Building Your Mate's Self-Esteem, by Dennis and Barbara Rainey.
- Ten Questions Every Husband Should Ask His Wife Every Year, by Tom and Jeannie Elliff, http://www.familylife.com/articles/topics/marriage/staying-married/husbands/10-questions-to-ask-your-wife-every-year#.Uvl6CmJdWSo.
- Ten Questions Every Wife Should Ask Her Husband Every Year, by Tom and Jeannie Elliff, http://www.familylife.com/articles/topics/marriage/staying-married/communication/10-questions-every-woman-should-ask-her-husband-every-year#.Uvl6P2JdWSo.
- Sacred Marriage, by Gary Thomas.
- For Men ONLY, by Jeff and Shaunti Feldhahn.
- For Women ONLY, by Shaunti Feldhahn.
- 10 Surprising Ways to Increase Romance, by Sabrina Beasley, http://www.familylife.com/articles/topics/marriage/staying-married/romance-and-sex/10-surprising-ways-to-increase-romance#.Uvl8mmJdWSo.
- The Peacemaker: A Biblical Guide to Resolving Personal Conflict, by Ken Sande. See Chapter 1 for more information on the Four G's – A Theology for Conflict Resolution.
- Six Steps for Resolving Conflict in Marriage, by Dennis and Barbara Rainey, http://www.familylife.com/site/apps/nlnet/content3.aspx?c=dnJHKLNnFoG&b=3871749&ct=4639663.